SIMPLE

SIMPLE C
A Beginner's Guide

Ian Sinclair

David Fulton Publishers

London

David Fulton Publishers Ltd
14 Chalton Drive, London N2 0QW

First published in Great Britain by
David Fulton Publishers 1988

British Library Cataloguing in Publication Data
Sinclair, Ian R. (Ian Robertson), *1932–*
  Simple C: a beginner's guide.
  1. Microcomputer systems. Programming
  languages. Simple C language
  I. Title
  005.2'6

  ISBN 1–85346–057–5

Typeset by Chapterhouse, The Cloisters, Formby, L37 3PX
Printed and bound in Great Britain
by Biddles Ltd. Guildford

Contents

Preface

This book is intended for the true beginner to programming in C on the PC. There are many books on the C language, all of which to some extent owe their material to the source book, *The C Programming Language*, by Kernighan and Ritchie. Kernighan and Ritchie's book is a definitive statement of the C language, as well it should be since Ritchie is the originator of C, and anything that differs from that version has to be regarded with suspicion. The exceptions to this rule are the amendments made by the ANSI standardising committee, and this book includes the most recent of these amendments.

The K & R book, as it is affectionately known, is not in any sense a book for the beginner to computing languages, and is a reference book rather than a way of learning the language. This text, by contrast, is an attempt to introduce you in a much more gently guided way to this very significant and useful language. This means that the language is not exhaustively described in every possible detail, nor is every possible combination of statements explored. The aim is to get you thinking in C so that you can start writing programs for yourself as soon as possible. Once you have made this start and no longer think of C as a strange alien language you will be ready for the more advanced aspects of C, and it is then that you need to have K & R handy.

Although C is a very portable language in the sense that a correctly written C program should run on any machine that can run a C compiler, it is always easier to write descriptions that apply to one particular machine. Since the Amstrad PC is now so widely used, and other PCs are totally compatible as far as C is concerned, this book deals with C on the PC. There are many excellent versions of C compilers for the PC, and I have used Zorland C to compile the examples. The descriptions of compiling and linking in this book apply, therefore, to Zorland C on the PC, but are so representative of other systems that I thought it better to describe a specific example rather than to leave a vague instruction of the form 'consult your manual'.

What I have attempted to do is to introduce C to the reader who has probably programmed to some extent in the universal language, BASIC, and to show the few similarities and the very many differences between these languages. I hope that in the course of doing this I have illustrated how flexible, useful and beautiful the language is. Once you have worked your way through this book and, more importantly, worked with the examples on your own computer and tried out some ideas of your own, then if you are serious about C you should buy a copy of K & R to act as the ultimate reference.

I am most grateful to David Fulton for his interest in this project, and to John Haggins of Zorland Ltd for the long-term loan of the Zorland compiler and the many library sets that Zorland supply to support their C system. I have also seen many other compilers and manuals in the course of writing this book, and I am most grateful to the many suppliers of compilers who have been patient in the face of my persistent questions.

Ian Sinclair, February 1988

1
What is C?

C is the curiously short name for one of the great computing languages of our time. The name is an historical accident, as I'll show you later, but for now we'll concentrate on the what and the why of it.

To start with, we have to look at programming languages generally and ask just what is it that we require of languages. At the bottom of the heap of programming level comes *machine code*, written directly in binary or hex digits. Machine-code programming is tedious, error-prone, and liable to hold a bug in every byte. There are three main reasons for using it. One is that it is the only way to program a completely new microprocessor for which nothing is written. Another is its speed, and the third is to achieve tighter control over the computer. The first reason applies only if you design and write language compilers for new microprocessors, but the other two are the reasons that keep machine code programmers in business. Machine code is fast; there is nothing faster, and for some types of programming, notably animated graphics, this speed is essential. The third reason is also important: there are always features of a machine that can be controlled only by machine code. No language, and particularly a language such as BASIC, can ever cope with every possibility that a programmer might want. If you want to have your screen scrolling diagonally, or to read a disk that is abnormally formatted, or use a non-standard printer, then you need machine code to write the routines.

There is such a continuing need for machine code that we need a programming language, *assembly language*, for each microprocessor type in order to write machine code with less tedium and fewer bugs. Assembly language, then, comes slightly higher up the scale as compared to machine code because it is easier to write, but it still translates directly to machine code.

What about the other end of the scale? There is one high level language, COBOL, which, when you read a program written in this language, looks almost like a set of instructions in English. When you write programs in a language like this you don't expect to have to worry about the details of the machine that you are using. You aren't interested in what processor it uses (it might be a mainframe with a central processor unit which is not a microprocessor chip), or how many bits make a byte or what address is used for the printer port. You don't need to know ASCII codes or routines in the ROM (if any) or any of the things that constantly occupy the minds of assembly language programmers. You simply write your program lines, run them into the machine, compile, and sit back like anyone else until the compilation fails. The language processor, invariably a compiler, converts the instructions of your program into machine code and the computer can then execute the machine code.

The name *high-level* is a good one. You are so far above the ground level of machine code that you hardly know there's a machine present. Needless to say, a language like this should be the same no matter on what computer the program is intended to run. The language is portable – but that doesn't mean that you can pick it up easily. Between the heights of COBOL and two other old-established languages, FOR-TRAN and ALGOL, and the depths of machine code, there are languages at all sorts of intermediate levels.

The fundamental problem is that high level languages are powerful but inefficient. They allow you to turn your problem-solving methods into programs that run smoothly but at a great cost in memory space. They can be cumbersome, using lines and lines of program which can take all day to compile even if the program runs fairly quickly once compiled. At the other end of the scale, machine code is very compact, very fast and very efficient, but sheer hell to write and debug in any quantity. In addition, a program written in assembly language has to be very carefully documented if there is to be any chance of modifying it at a later date, or if anyone else might have to work with it.

The reason that we have such a large number of programming languages is that we are constantly trying to get a better balance of these different virtues. What we want is a high level language that makes it easy to express our solutions to problems, is very compact both in statement length and its use of memory, and which translates into as few bytes of machine code as would be provided by an assembler. There is no such language, and probably never will be, but some languages come nearer to the ideal than others, and some are a better solution for some specific types of problems. For example, a lot of programming of the type used in robotics is well handled by the language FORTH, but you would want a truck load of aspirin if you intended to write a word-processor in FORTH – and who ever saw a job advertisement for FORTH programmers?

The history of computing, then, is littered with languages which seemed to be a good idea at the time or which looked like being a good solution to one type of need. The greatest computing languages are the ones which have incorporated ideas that have lasted and have passed into other languages in turn. For example, one of the first great languages (still in use) was FORTRAN, and its principles have been so absorbed into BASIC that a FORTRAN programmer can easily switch to BASIC without feeling that this is a radically different type of language. The other great language of the early computing days is ALGOL, and that is where we start the story of the development of C.

The name of C is almost an accident, derived from the history of the language. A remote ancestor of C was a language called CPL, meaning Combined Progamming Language. This was evolved around around 1963 in the Universities of Cambridge and London as an attempt to make a more practical version of ALGOL which would incorporate some of the features of FORTRAN.

ALGOL is a very different type of language as compared to FORTRAN or BASIC. It's one of the first of the modern style of computing languages and one which did not find much favour among commercial programmers in its day. Looking back, it's not easy to see why ALGOL was so rejected, and modern versions are still regarded as being among the most effective computer languages for large machines. One reason given at the time was that ALGOL seemed too much of a general-purpose language, unlike FORTRAN or COBOL. FORTRAN (an acronym for FORmula TRANslation) was specifically designed for scientific, technical and mathematical use, and COBOL (COmmon Business Oriented Language) was designed to cope with the requirements of accounting, stock control and office practices.

In any case, CPL fared little better in the popularity stakes because it ended up as a big language that needed a lot of memory for its compiler. It also contained a large number of statement actions that required a lot of effort to learn and many of these were not necessarily particularly useful to the commercial programmer. The ideas that had passed from ALGOL to CPL, however, were too good to be allowed to lapse, and Martin Richards at Cambridge came up with a new version in 1967 and named it BCPL, with B meaning Basic in the sense of simplified.

The aim of BCPL was to create a compact language that could be used by machines with small memory capacities – and you should remember at this point that a lot of mainframe machines at the time had quite small memory capacities by modern standards. BCPL retained the best features of CPL, and is still available for a few machines whose memory capacity is not up to running C, but both BCPL, and a later variant, B, suffer from being too brief. When a language becomes too brief (like the early 4K BASIC versions that we once thought were so handy) it becomes too limited for really effective programming. You find that there is no command to do what you want, and end up writing ten lines of program just to accomplish one simple action. At the other end of the scale, some modern versions of BASIC have become completely over-blown, requiring you to know some 200-plus instruction words in order to program for a wide variety of purposes.

The significance of B in this story, however, is that it was written at Bell Laboratories by Ken Thompson in 1970, a time when the UNIX operating system was being developed for mainframe computers. Work-ing also at Bell Laboratories was Dennis Ritchie and in 1972, at the start of the microprocessor age, he invented C, just one year before Gary Kildall devised the CP/M operating system. The name of C was simply to indicate a follow-on to B, and the aim of the language was to create a method of writing operating systems and utilities to work with UNIX. UNIX was still under development, and there was an urgent need for something faster than assembly language which could be used to speed up the development of the system.

C is a language which is at a level midway between COBOL and machine code. It is an economical language, meaning that a few short statements can accomplish a lot of action. It's also a language that is very rich in control structures so that you can form loops easily and escape from them easily, without the use of GOTO. It also has a good range of data types so that you can work with any type of data, number, character, string array and so on. Its main glory, however, is that it is remarkably free from the restrictions that a lot of high-level languages place on the programmer. It's a programmers' language rather than an academics' language.

Just to give an example of what I mean by this, traditional PASCAL allows you to define a string as being an array of a given number of characters, a method of dealing with strings that is used by most languages (including C) other than BASIC. If you define NAME in traditional PASCAL as being a string of ten characters, then you can't assign the name SINCLAIR to the variable NAME because there are only eight characters in SINCLAIR. To make the assignment work, you have to add two spaces to SINCLAIR so as to make the length up to the required ten characters. This is a type of restriction which is unknown in BASIC and which is also much less of a problem in C (and in modern versions of PASCAL and in its successor, MODULA-2). This absence of restrictions makes C a very useful language for programmers who are working with machine utilities and systems, but such a lack of restrictions is bought at a price.

C will allow you to do practically anything, and that includes making silly mistakes. Hand in hand with the lack of restrictions goes a lack of checks. As long as your syntax looks reasonable you can make any mis-take you like and you will not know anything about it until your program crashes. Even seasoned C programmers can put very elusive bugs into programs; in fact the more experienced you get the more elusive your bugs become. Given the choice, though, most programmers will accept the risks in order to write more efficient programs. Nothing is ever perfect. You might not cut yourself on a blunt chisel, but it's not much use on wood. Given the choice, craftsmen choose sharp chisels and learn to use them correctly. In computing terms, C is a very sharp chisel, and the improvements of the ANSI committee have added a few protections that avoid some types of disaster without getting in the way.

Compilers and interpreters

Like many other languages, C can be obtained in a compiled or an interpreted form. Whatever language you use to express your program ideas in, it has to be converted into machine code before it can be used in the computer. Interpreting and compiling are two different methods of carrying out this conversion, and if you have used only BASIC–2 on the Amstrad PC, or BASICA on other PCs, you will probably be familiar only with *interpreting*. When a language is interpreted, each instruction is taken in turn as the interpreter comes to it. The instruction is checked to find if it is valid, and then it is executed by calling up a machine-code subroutine. In practical terms, this means that a complete set of machine-code subroutines must exist on disk, in the RAM, or in ROM, and each reserved word of the language will call up a routine or a set of routines. In a loop, for example, each instruction in the loop will be interpreted, checked and run on each pass through the loop, and it is this need to interpret and check on each occasion that makes a BASIC interpreter so slow in action.

A *compiled language*, by contrast, converts all of the instructions of a program into a large machine-code program. At first sight, this looks very like the same type of action as interpreting. The difference is most easily understood if we look at how a *compiler* would deal with a loop. In this case, the validity of the instructions needs to be checked once, the machine-code for the loop action collected, and a machine code loop set up. The finding and collecting of code is done once only, not in each pass of the loop. The result of compiling is usually recorded on disk rather than being run at the time (though some compilers will compile to RAM and allow you to run the result). Once a program has been compiled, it consists of a set of machine-code routines, and these have then to be linked together and into the routines of the operating system, which for PC machines means MS-DOS or PC-DOS. If the compiler is a good one, then the machine code may be almost as compact as it would have been if it had been created by an assembler (referred to as native machine code).

Nothing is perfect, and both interpreters and compilers have merits and faults. The main merit of an interpreter is easy debugging. When your interpreted program stops with an error message you can change the program text and try again. For a compiled program, which would mean loading in the text, compiling it, linking it and then running again, which is inevitably a slower process. The disadvantage of the interpreter is low speed, because the process of finding the machine-code routines can be a lengthy one, and it has to be done each time an instruction is obeyed. The ease of use of the interpreter is paid for by slow running, and the high speed of the compiler is paid for by the expense of easy checking and changing.

For most purposes, however, the use of a compiler is a considerable advantage. Even if you write programs only for your own uses, it's a nuisance to have to load in an interpreter before you can run a program. If you write programs for sale to others (or to put into the public domain) the use of a compiler is almost essential. For one thing, it's usually easier to protect machine-code programs against copying if you feel that you must do so. More important is that you retain some control. Since you keep the *source code* (the text that was compiled to create the machine code) you can alter the text, recompile, and issue new versions. Others, lacking your source code, cannot modify your program so easily. The main advantage, however, is that a compiler allows you to write programs in a high level language but operate with fast-running machine-code. For learning C an interpreter (such as the excellent Living C) is very useful, but for writing serious programs in C, a good compiler is essential.

Outline of C

Unless you know more than one programming language, it is always very difficult to explain what it is about a new language that makes it useful. It is rather like explaining the colour green to someone who is completely colour-blind. Unless you have some notion of what can be achieved, it's difficult to imagine how one language can be so very different from another.

This is particularly true if you have only ever programmed in BASIC, because BASIC was devised as a beginner's language modelled on one of the oldest languages, FORTRAN. The aim, in fact, was to introduce the beginner to programming in a language that looked similar to FOR-TRAN so that FORTRAN could be introduced more painlessly. If you have used a very advanced version of BASIC (meaning one that is not very like BASIC as it was originally conceived), such as BASIC–2 or BASICA, then the task is easier. If you have used a structured language like PASCAL or MODULA–2, then it is easier still. Even if your only other language is assembler, it still becomes easier to understand the ideas of C. The advantages can be summed up as structure, compactness and portability.

Structure is the idea that is most difficult to get over to programmers who have used only BASIC. This is more often because of the way that BASIC is learned, by accident and experiment rather than by design. A structured program is one that has been rationally designed using *structures* like statement groups, IF...THEN...ELSE decisions, and WHILE loops. The most important point is the absence of anything that resembles a GOTO.

Any program is a solution to a problem, whether it's to analyse the tax affairs of a business or to write a letter to your Uncle Toby. In a structured program, the solution is easy to follow because the program has been split into manageable sections and each section is dealt with by similar methods. An unstructured program, by contrast, is very difficult to follow because you can't see the process of solution, you can't see how one step leads to another.

Most high level languages are almost unusable unless you design your programs to have some structure, and BASIC is the one big exception to this rule. You can write a program in BASIC which starts with printing the answer to a problem, goes on to inputting the quantities that are to be processed, and then the processing of these quantities to find the solution. How do you make it work? Easy, just stick in GOTOs until it does work. The result looks a mess, is usually full of unexpected bugs and is almost impossible to extend improve or adjust. BASIC programming doesn't have to be like that and even in a version of BASIC that is comparatively primitive it is possible to write programs that have some structure, by making use of a lot of subroutines.

The trouble is that BASIC was never designed as a structured language, and most versions lack the statements that would make it a really structured language. In any case, if it had all these things, it would not really be BASIC – it would probably be something like COMAL. Unlike BASIC, C is structured, but not to the point of forcing you along restricted paths so that you yearn for a couple of quick GOTOs just to relieve the monotony. Along with structure goes *modularity*. A *modular language* is one in which you can break down any program into small units or *modules* and work on these independently. This is probably the greatest difference between BASIC and other languages, because the subroutines of most varieties of BASIC are not truly modular. The main feature of a truly modular language is that the modules can be independent of each other and of the main program, which implies local variables.

To illustrate what I mean, imagine a BASIC subroutine which is called up by the statement GOSUB 1000 and which uses the variable A%. If A% is used in the main program, then the subroutine can also use this variable name and can alter the value that is assigned to it. This altered value can also be used in the main program, because it is *global* – altering the value of A% anywhere in the program alters the value for all other parts also. When you design a BASIC program, then, you have to organise the design of subroutines very carefully, specifying variable names that will not cause problems elsewhere. This can mean that a lot of effort is spent in copying values from one variable name to another, and the use of a very large number of variable names.

By contrast, in C, all of the variables in a *function*, the equivalent of a subroutine, are local. If you have a variable called A in a function, then a value allocated to it in that function exists only in that function. It does not have the same value as a variable called A which exists in the main program, or a variable called A which exists in any other function, nor can it affect these values.

It is only by very deliberate programming steps that you can pass a value into a function or pass a value back from a function. This makes it possible to design each module separately without having to worry about what variable names will have been used in the main program, what values they have and what will happen if these values are changed. Each module is a little island unto itself, and you have complete control over immigration and emigration. That's modularity.

The third feature of C is portability, which means that programs written on one machine can be used on another, though this may mean recompiling. No-one is likely to claim that BASIC is a portable language, because a program written in BASIC for one machine is most unlikely to run on another without a lot of modification. I don't just mean that a disk made by one machine will not run on another because unless you use eight inch disks that is a normal situation. The problem of portability in BASIC is that even a listing prepared with one machine will not necessarily run on another, though this is less of a problem with the PC type of machine.

It is possible to write programs in a subset of BASIC, meaning a few commands that are common to all dialects of BASIC, But programming in this way is like trying to write in English using only the 50 most common words. By contrast, if you have a program listing in C, then it should run, given a few conditions, in almost any machine that can make use of a suitable C compiler. That's portability!

The conditions are fairly obvious ones. The compiler must allow all of the normal statements of C. Some compilers for small machines, or the simpler types of compilers, do not allow the use of floating-point numbers, meaning numbers that include fractions. If a program includes graphics or other screen effects, then it will run correctly only on a computer that uses the same screen codes or for which suitable library functions are available. In the main, though, it is the compatibility of compilers rather than the compatibility of machines that matters. What you can be sure of is that your version of C will be portable for writing systems programs. This is the job for which C was originally intended for and it's what C does best. In addition, if you happen to be using a machine that runs the UNIX operating system, then your C programs will match the operating system like bacon matches eggs.

If you are using the PC machine, then the operating system that you are familiar with is MS-DOS (or PC-DOS). The operating system provides the input and output routines so that you can make use of disk drives, printers, keyboard and VDU. It manages the memory of the machine so that your programs can be located and run, and it should also provide a set of utilities that can make programming easier. The distinguishing feature of UNIX is that it was originally designed for very large machines, and so it needs a lot of memory. In this book, we shall be looking only at the use of C in the MS-DOS system of the PC.

If you had to make a quick summary of what C had to offer, you could make it in this phrase: C is a language which combines the power of machine-code with the structure of a high level language. In longer terms, C allows you the control over what the computer does that you normally associate with machine-code, and will generate compiled code that is almost as compact as machine-code from an assembler. At the same time, though, C provides all the structures of a good high level language, like the facilities for creating loops, many different variable types, structured variables like arrays, and so on. If you have worked only with BASIC, a lot of these advantages will be almost unimaginable. You can, however, grasp another C advantage, the compacting of code.

It is possible to write C in perfectly correct form, and then to make the program considerably shorter by making some adjustments. Most of the statements of C can be written in a way that is not just shorter to read but which compiles faster and gives faster running code. In BASIC, you probably know dodges like using integer variables in FOR ... NEXT loops, using short variable names, omitting words like LET and so on. These are just minor trimmings compared to the way that a C program can be shortened and speeded up.

Another major difference is in the number of reserved words of the language. The tendency in recent years has been to bigger BASIC interpreters, allowing for 150 or more reserved words to be used. When you use C, you will be struck by how few reserved words exist. The difference is that C is a small language with few reserved words. Instead of making the language contain a huge number of words for actions, C contains only the minimum necessary.

The other actions that you are likely to need are supplied in the form of functions (usually compiled ready to use), collected into a library. You are not stuck with the library of functions that you get along with your compiler either, because you can buy additional libraries, and also add functions to the library for yourself. It is because the core part of C is small that the language is so portable, and the library system is what makes C so very useful. It's rather like having a BASIC of 30 reserved words but with several hundred subroutines on a disk that you could incorporate into your programs. To use C to best advantage, then, you have to know what is in your library or libraries, and how you can add to this.

How, then, do you start? There are some public-domain C interpreters and compilers if you just want a flavour of the language, but if you are more serious, then a full-scale commercial compiler is a must. This need not be expensive, and I am using the Zorland compiler for the Amstrad machine, with an all-up price of under £30. At the time of writing, this included the all-important linker program which was not supplied with the Amstrad package. In this book, the programs which are illustrated can be run using the compiler to create the smallest memory model. The PC machine is designed in such a way that programs can be created either to make use of 64K or less, or to spread into more of the memory at the cost of slower running. C compilers are therefore designed to cater for several sizes of memory use. By using only the smallest mode, you can ignore the complications that attend the use of extended memory, and can therefore concentrate on learning C rather than learning to cope with the complexities of the PC's memory system. Details of compiling and linking with the Zorland compiler will be explained when we come to a sample program. Other compilers broadly follow a similar pattern, so that it should not require too much consultation of a manual if you are using any other modern C compiler.

2
Principles

Every programming language is based on a few important principles, and C is no exception. In BASIC, you are used to the idea that your program uses line numbers and that statements are executed in order of ascending line number unless a GOTO or other redirection decided otherwise. You can forget most of the principles of BASIC when you start to work with C, because the language is quite different. For one thing, you don't use line numbers. The main part of the program is written with everything in correct order so that line numbers are not needed. Instead of calling a subroutine with a line number (like GOSUB 1000) you call a function with a name (like sortit). At first sight, this makes a program in C look more difficult to follow, like a country road with all the signs removed. We'll look in more detail at all this in the following chapters, but for the moment there are two other important points about C.

One is that it can use *compound statements*, meaning a collection of statements that behave like one single statement. In BASIC, the nearest you get to this is a collection of related instructions gathered into one line with colons separating the parts, something like:

        100 INPUT A:PRINT A:PRINT#5,A

in which all the actions concern the same variable. The other point is that C contains a lot more methods of controlling the flow of a program. There are extended IF tests, for example, using ELSE. There are several different types of loops, allowing you to test for the ending condition of a loop at any point in the loop, to jump cleanly out of a loop, or even to ignore one pass through a loop and go on to the next. These are the structures of C, and they are the items that make C so unlike most versions of BASIC. Once you know what to look for, you'll find that a program written in C is, in fact, easier to follow than one in BASIC. The most important difference, though, is in structure.

Program structure

The structure of a program means how it is arranged and organised into orderly units. Some BASIC programs are about as structured as the path of a drunken fly. Others are neatly arranged with a simple main core program which calls subroutines to perform the actions of the main program. If you have written programs of the core-and-subroutine type, as you are encouraged to do in BASIC–2 or BASICA, then it's likely that you'll take well to C. If your programs have been of the 'fly-track' variety, you will have real problems! C forces you to have some structure about your programs, and the type of structure is one that is far removed from BASIC. For example, in some varieties of BASIC, you might call up a subroutine in a line like:

    220 GOSUB 5000:PRINT A%;

which carries out a subroutine, prints the value of an integer number, and keeps the printing in the same line.

This could never be mistaken for a program written in C. For one thing, lines in a C listing aren't normally numbered, although some C compiler editors use line numbering for your convenience in editing. If you write the lines in the correct order, the order that the compiler will deal with them, there's no need for line numbers. The second point is that the subroutine starts somewhere later in the program, at line 5000. We can't have such a thing in C, because the compiler can't use line numbers. Instead of using a subroutine which is called by its line number, C uses a function which is called by using its name. Users of BASIC–2 on the Amstrad PC are familiar with this idea, and the principle is developed further in C. Even the instruction PRINT is not used in C, and the semicolon does not mean 'don't take a new line'. Did I really say that knowing one computer language would prepare you for another?

The point that is really important here, though, is order. In BASIC, you can write a core program which has calls to subroutines. It won't run correctly until the subroutines have been entered, but you can place the subroutines anywhere you like in the program. By contrast, defined functions in many varieties of BASIC must be placed ahead of the point at which they are called. If you have a function which, for example, multiplies a price by 0.15 so as to work out the amount of VAT, you must, in most varieties of BASIC, define it before you use it. You can have lines in BASIC such as:

    10 DEF FNVat(S) = S*.15
    20 INPUT "BASE PRICE";X
    30 PRINT"VAT IS ";FNVat(X)

because the BASIC interpreter can't look ahead for FNVat. The similarity here is that a defined function in BASIC is called into action by using its name, FNVat in this example, rather than by using a line number. In a C program all functions must be defined, but this can be done following the main program or ahead of it, providing we follow the rules of C. Like a well-structured BASIC program then, which might consist of a core program of perhaps ten to a hundred lines of main program followed by subroutines, a C program is written in the order of *main*, the main function or core program, and then the other functions. This means that details, such as declaring variable types, all come at the start of the program, followed by the main program, and the other functions often come last of all. This is a very logical arrangement as far as the programmer is concerned, and it makes the writing of programs much simpler than is the case in other languages. Any modern version of C can be expected to possess a good editing system, so it's easy to add statements at the start or at the end of a program if you have left something out.

The structure of a program in C follows the principle of *top-down* programming, often used as another name for structured programming. The principle is to break a problem down into outline and detail. The outline shows the main steps that are required to solve a problem, and the order in which these must be carried out. The details are then worked out for each main step, and this in turn may lead to another set of details. The top of the problem is the outline, the bottom is the finest detail. The way that C is constructed encourages you, almost forces you, to construct your programs in this form. As you progress through this book you will see how this idea operates and this, along with some experience of using C, will give you a much better idea of what is involved than any amount of reading about it.

Another part of C that is tied up with structure is the use of the library, something else that we'll look at in detail later. The C language is a small one, with very few reserved words as compared to any modern BASIC. This is because structured programming hinges on the use of functions to carry out the details, and these functions, being applicable to any program (no line numbers, all variables local) can be recorded on a disk or a set of disks. These disks then form the C library, with each function acting as an extension of the language. Just as you can put together a BASIC program by using its keywords, you can put together a C program by making use of its library functions. In addition, though, you can extend the library for yourself with your own functions, so extending the language. This library system is possible only because C is modular and because functions can be written with purely local variables.

The order of things

C is not simply a structured, modular, portable compiled (or interpreted) language, it is a language in which programs can be written which compile to unusually compact and fast machine-code. Once again, this is possible only if you program in the correct order, though. The most important idea to get used to, if your programming experience is in BASIC, is that types of variables and their names have to be declared before they can be used. In BASIC, you can write a line like:

100 A% = 5

which introduces a variable name, A%, with the % sign meaning that this is an *integer*. At the same time, the value to which A% is assigned is made equal to 5. A C programmer can write a very similar kind of line, but it has to appear early in a program, before the variable will be used. The C form of this line will be:

int a = 5;

with *int* used instead of the % sign to mean that 'a' represents an integer. Using this declaration means that we use only 'a' in the program, not 'int a' or 'a%'. The use of the equality sign and the 5 then assigns a value of 5 to a. The assignment does not have to be made here, it can be done later in the program. Declaring a variable type, and assigning a value in one step is just one of the short cuts that C allows and which makes it such a very interesting and challenging language. The semicolon at the end of the line marks the end of this statement.

This idea of declaring what type of variable is represented is not one that appears much in BASIC. The PC machines can use BASICA, GW BASIC or QBASIC which allow instructions such as DEFINT. This allows you to define how letters will be used in the program. For example, DEFINT A–D in GW BASIC means that any variable name which starts with the letters A, B, C, or D will be an integer variable. This means that you no longer have to mark integer variables, like A%, BY%, COWS% and so on, to show that they are integers. The DEFINT statement at the start of the program has done this for you, and it's also possible to define string or real-number variables in a similar way.

In C, however, this idea of declaring how names will be used in advance is all-important, though different in style. Note, too, that I said 'names'. In BASIC–2 and other BASICs for the PC, you are probably used to working with variable 'names' like Apple, Belong$ and so on. C also allows you to use realistic names of this style rather than just letters singly or in pairs. This is an advantage in C, because using long names in a compiled program does not slow down the action of the program as it does with interpreted BASIC. You must, however, define what type of item each name will be used for. This allows the compiler to prepare for each variable that will be used by making the correct allocation of memory. You cannot write statements which in BASIC look like:

NAME = "SINCLAIR"

4444444444

in C unless you have, earlier in the program, declared that NAME is a variable that will be used for a string of at least nine characters. Nine has to be used for an eight-letter name, because in C, a string must end with a zero, which is the ninth character. You can't make this declaration later, because the compiler will halt when it finds a name used that it has no notification about. You cannot ever use a name unless you have defined the name. The definition does not necessarily need to be placed at the start of the program, but it certainly must come before you attempt to use the name. So that I don't have to use long-winded phrases each time I remind you of this idea, I'll give it its correct name from now on – it's called *pre-declaration*.

To a BASIC programmer, it may seem odd that you can find a variable called NAME and not have any mark (like $ or %) to tell you what kind of variable it is. Once you get used to C, though, you will find that it is more natural to start off a program with a list of the variable names that will be used. This is another aspect of structure; you need to have planned these names in advance rather than just put them in at a moment's notice. It's only too easy in a long and poorly planned BASIC program to use a variable name more than once without realising it, and so causing a very obscure bug. You can't do that sort of thing in C, or in any other structured language.

First steps

All C programs can be constructed in the same way, and though you can leave out some steps in certain versions, it's advisable to keep to the rules of standard C. If you do it's much easier to write C programs for practically any machine. In addition, it helps a lot if you write programs the way that you ought to design them, outline first and details later. Remember also that you need to keep to the rules of the machine you are using as well. Any features of a particular machine or compilers that you are using should be listed prominently in the manual that comes with the compiler, and it's likely that you will know the eccentricities of your machine by the time you take up C programming in any case. Those of us who use the Amstrad PC tend to think of other machines as being the odd ones! Users of Zorland C, however, will never be likely to encounter problems of non-standard features.

Getting back to program construction, though, the layout order of a program in C is one of definitions, main function, and then functions that are called by the main function. The main function is marked by the use of the word main (), and the extent of this main function is marked by the use of curly brackets, one to open the main function and the other to close it.

The simplest possible outline of a real C program then, apart from the traditional 'Hello, world' type, is:

```
various definitions
main()
{
declarations for main
the main function
}
functions called by main or by other functions
```

and in this brief outline of a program there is quite a lot to assimilate. To start with, there can be quite a lot of material preceding the main function. You can, if you like, put all the other functions preceding main, as many programmers do, and there will be some functions that must be placed before main unless some alterations are made to the way in which these functions are called. In addition, definitions are placed here, before the start of main.

A definition in this sense refers to a word which will have a special meaning in the program. You might, for example, be reading files into your program, and so you will need to define what is meant by EOF, the end of file marker. On most machines this is -1, so you would define EOF as meaning -1 and in your program use EOF wherever it was needed rather than -1. This has two advantages. One is that if you have to adapt your C program to a machine that uses a different value for the end of file marker then the change is made by editing just one line, the definition line. The other advantage is that it is a lot easier to see what is happening in the program if you use abbreviations like EOF rather than numbers like -1, particularly if there is any chance that a -1 will crop up anywhere else used in a different way. The most common of these definitions are gathered into groups and used in conjunction with your library as #include files, of which more later.

The next point is that the word main needs to be followed immediately (no spaces) by a pair of round brackets. The brackets are an essential part of this, and it's not very often that you need to put anything between these brackets. For other names of functions, though, you will want to place various items between the brackets to contain the variable names for values that will be passed to the function. There may be times when you do need to put something between the brackets of main. This will arise when you call a program and at the same time pass some values to it, and the details of this are noted in Chapter 11. In any case, you can't omit the brackets, because main is a function like any other function, and all function names must be followed by brackets. The only thing that distinguishes main from other functions, in fact, is that a C program must contain one and only one main, even if no other functions are used. Following the main () entry, a new line is taken.

The next feature is the set of declarations that apply to main. These declarations will include each variable name that will be used in main, and possibly some of the variables that will be used in other functions. The difference is one that we'll look at later, distinguishing between global and local variables. As well as declaring the names that will be used, the type of variable must be declared. We'll look at variable types shortly, but the principle is that you have to state a variable type and then list what names are of this type. If you are using integers, for example, you declare the type integer and then list all the names that you will use for integer variables. Some of the variables that you declare in this section may be far from simple, like arrays and structures, and we'll look at these later.

The main function then starts with a curly bracket (or brace) and will end with the opposite facing curly bracket. Between these brackets (usually placed on a line by themselves) you may have various statements, and some of these may use curly brackets so that the brackets will be nested. As in any nesting, you have to be sure that the nesting order is correct and there are as many closing curly brackets as there are opening curly brackets. This should not be difficult to ensure if your programs are correctly written. In a correctly written C program, the actions of the program should be split into small groups each of which can be carried out by a separate function. The main function should therefore be short and since it is short it is not difficult to check the nesting of curly brackets.

In general, if any piece of a program takes more than a page to list you haven't really planned it too well. The whole point in having a modular language is so that you can work in modules of convenient size, and a page is convenient in the sense that you can look at a page at a time. You should never, looking at a C listing, get that feeling of helplessness that you get when you are holding three metres of a listing in BASIC and you find that the first line is:

```
10 GOTO 10515
```

Now, having looked at the outline of the construction of main, what does each other function look like? The answer is 'almost identical', and the only essential is the use of another name, because there can be only one main. If your function name is *getinput*, for example, then the function will have this name with its round brackets following. Within these brackets you would have the names of any variables whose values (not the variables, notice, only the values) will be used inside the function, so that a function called getinput might appear as:

```
getinput(namel,name2);
```

where namel and name2 are variables whose values will be used inside the function. Following the title, these variable names must be declared in the usual way, then an opening curly bracket announces the start of the function. More variables might be declared at this stage to be used inside the function. The actions of the function follow and if any variable value has to be returned from the function this is done using a return statement. This is *not* like the use of RETURN in a BASIC subroutine, though it has the same effect of forcing the function to return control to wherever it was called from. For one thing, the return of C usually specifies a variable whose value is to be returned; for another the function will return even if there is no return statement. The closing curly bracket of a function marks the end, and a function will return at this point if there has been no separate return statement.

As you can see, the construction is almost identical to that of main, except that for most of the other functions there will be a variable name or names placed between the round brackets, and these names are used to pass values to the functions. If you have used only subroutines in BASIC, this is something that will be very new to you. Suppose, to take an example, that you had a program which dealt in words and at some point in the program you wanted to call up a routine to put a word into capital letters. In BASIC, you might represent the word by the variable name WD$, and you would use a subroutine which changed the contents of WD$. This new value of WD$ would then be available to be used by the rest of the program. In this example, WD$ is a variable that is used in the main core program and in the subroutine, its value is available in both and it can be changed in either. It is, in short, a global variable.

Things could hardly be more different in C. We can create global variables, and an illustration will be dealt with later, but we seldom choose to use them. Unless we choose to make use of global variables whose value is maintained in all sections of the program, no quantity that exists in the form of a variable in the main function can be used in another function unless the value is passed to that function. Being passed means that the value is held in a variable name which is placed between the round brackets in the function name. For example, if we used the variable name of word to hold a string of letters, then this could be used in a function makecap only by calling the function in the form:

    makecap(word);

and if word is omitted, then the function has no argument, nothing to work on.

There is another difference. If the function makes some changes to the value of word this will not necessarily cause any change to the value that is held by word in the main program. For example, if word represents 'Figment', and this is changed in the function to FIGMENT, then after the function has run the variable name of word will still contain 'Figment'. This is because only the value of a variable is passed to a function, not the variable name, and unless some steps are taken to pass a changed values back and reassign it to the variable, the original value will remain. If a value of a variable is to be changed by a function, then rather more specialised methods have to be used.

As far as each function is concerned, it operates in a little world of its own. Whatever quantities are passed to it it can use, modify, print and perhaps pass to other functions, but this has nothing to do with any variable of the same name in the main program or in any other function. A variable like this is called *local*, and I am stressing it because unless you have programmed the BBC Micro in BASIC, you are most unlikely to have programmed using local variables in BASIC. C takes the idea of local variables much further, though, because in C all variables are normally local – we try to avoid global variables as far as possible. The purpose is an essential one; it allows you to design a function quite independently of the main program. Each function will be designed with its name, the name of variables that it will use (not necessarily the names that are used when the function is called) and its own set of actions. One person can design the main program, a different person can design each function, and the whole program can be put together with the minimum of fuss. Try that with BASIC!

This is what makes it possible to have a function library with a C compiler or on a separate disk. Each function is independent. If you have a function called toascii(c) and the c within the brackets means a single character code, then you can call this function from your main program with the line:

toascii(first)

providing that you have declared and used the variable name of first to mean a character. It's not the name that counts, it's the position in the brackets, so that first in the calling statement gets used in the way that we use c in the function definition. It is the equivalent of having a line in BASIC:

c = first

in order to pass the value from one variable to another.

If the function uses more than one variable, then the order must be correct when you call the function. For example, if you have a function convert(a,b,c) and you want to use this on variables J1, POINT2 and RANGE, then you have to call with:

convert(J1,POINT2,RANGE);

which means that in the function, a will be used to carry the value from J1, b will be used to carry the value from POINT2 and c will be used to carry the value from RANGE. The order has to be maintained, and the variables have to be declared as the correct types. This type of action is called *passing by value*.

Data types

In BASIC, you are accustomed to three *primary data types* (types of variables) and usually just one structured type. The simple data types are *integer number*, *floating-point number*, and *string*. In BASIC, these three different data types are represented by names with distinguishing marks used for integer and string types. For example, you could use the name AB for a floating-point number. AB% for an integer, and AB$ for a string. These are called primary data types because all the forms of data that you use must be expressed by one or other of these variable types. The only structured data type in most varieties of BASIC is the array. You can, for example use the name AB(0) to AB(10) to represent a set of eleven floating-point numbers in a number array. These numbers will be stored consecutively in the memory, which makes it easy for the computer to find any one member of the array provided that the address of the first member AB(0) is known.

Most varieties of BASIC allow string arrays as well, so that you can have arrays like WB$(0) to WB$(50) used in your programs. The reason for using the name *structured* for an array like this is that there is a structure of values stored in the memory of the computer and arranged so that the machine can get access to any part of that structure easily.

In C there is a much wider range of both primary and structured data types. Like BASIC, we can have floating-point numbers and integers, with the difference that the integers can be short, stored in two bytes, or long, stored in four bytes. Most C compilers allow another variety of

Type	Range
signed char	−128 to +127
char	0 to 255
int	−32768 to +32767
unsigned	0 to 65535
long	−2.15E9 to ~+2.15E9 approx.
unsigned long	0 to 4.3E9
float	−1E308 to +1E308 16 − digit precision
double	−1E308 to +1E308 16 − digit precision

Figure 2.1   The number types of C, with ranges. The larger ranges have been shown approximately.

integer, *unsigned*, and Fig. 2.1 shows the ranges of numbers that are usable with each type. The ordinary floating-point number variable is called a float, and there is a long version of this, called a double (or *double-precision number*). The use of doubles makes arithmetic much more precise but it slows down program action considerably unless you have the 8087 number-cruncher chip installed and have notified your C compiler of this. You would normally use doubles mainly for scientific and engineering calculations, but in fact most compilers will follow the rules of C and use double-precision for any arithmetic using floats. All of that accounts for three data types of which the integer can have three variations.

After that, things start to be very different. There is nothing corresponding to a string variable in C. The data type that we use when we are working with words is the *character*, which corresponds to a single ASCII code in BASIC. Since a character is an ASCII code, it can be stored in one byte and treated like a small integer. When we need to store a set of characters (a word or phrase) then we use an array of characters. This type of construction has been used in several varieties of BASIC in the past, notably in Atari and Sinclair machines.

There is another type of variable, the *pointer*, which performs much more in C than in BASIC or even in PASCAL. A pointer is an address for a variable rather than a data type, and for an eight-bit machine it is a two-byte integer. For the addressing system of the PC, because this is divided into 64K blocks, a two-byte pointer can also be used but for other 16-bit machines the pointer will consist of a greater number of bits. The value of a pointer is that it needs only these two bytes (or whatever) to refer to any other kind of variable, character or number, integer or float, single or double. Even more usefully, a pointer can refer to an array by holding the address of the first member of the array. The pointer is the means by which we can make a function change a quantity in the main program (or in any other function), and it's also the way in which we can tie ourselves into contorted knots if we are careless. We'll leave details of pointers until Chapter 7, pausing only to note that several of the varieties of BASIC for the PC use pointers in the form of the VARPTR statement.

The structured data types of C are the *array*, the *structure* and the *union*. The array is arranged very much like the array in BASIC, and you can have an array of any primary data type. The character array is rather special, because it is the equivalent of the BASIC string variable. For that reason, character arrays are used to a considerable extent. The other types, the structure and the union, have nothing remotely corresponding in BASIC and once again we'll leave them until later, in Chapter 10. The most common and useful data types of C are the character, the integer and the character array, and 95% or more of your programming is likely to use these types. If your compiler allows you to work with integers only (as the Zorland compiler optionally can), you can achieve a considerable reduction in program size by specifying this option for any program that does not require floating point numbers.

Getting started

To get started with C, you will need a compiler program, of which you have a large choice for most machines, except for some early types of machines with inadequate memory size. Certainly for all the machines in the PC class which run MS-DOS, the choice of C compilers and also of interpreters is almost embarrassingly large. The choice will often boil down to how much you can get for your money, and with packages like Zorland C on the market, the answer is a lot.

Your C package will include an *editor* with which you can create the text of a C program. Most editors use a similar command structure to that of WordStar on the assumption that everyone who uses a microcomputer will have used WordStar or a program with similar key actions. This is not necessarily true nowadays, but the editors that come with C compilers are generally simple to use if all you want to do is type, save and load text. At the beginner's level, the level of this book, this is indeed all that you need the editor for, so that if the commands are alien to you, it does not take long to pick up as much as you need. If you use Word-Star, you can create your C text by using WordStar in non-document mode, and if you use any other type of word-processor, then if it has the option of saving text in pure ASCII code this also can be used.

The stages in creating a program that has already been written are to type and save the text, compile the text (giving machine-code or object files), and then link this to the code that is needed to make your program run, meaning the runtime code and the MS-DOS system. For small C programs, many compiler packages allow the option of carrying out all the actions from the editor. This means that you can type the text, save it, and then carry out the compiling and linking in one action, and run the resulting code. This can represent a considerable saving in time when you are working with short programs (as in this book) or with short functions that you will later place into a library.

For longer programs, you can separate the editing action from the compiling and linking, and for the very longest programs, you can carry out the compiling (often two steps) and the linking in separate operations. The important point is that when you are learning C you don't want to get involved in lengthy compiling processes which distract you from the task in hand. The ideal compiler package, then, is one that allows you the option of simplicity for short programs, but allow also the options of creating very much larger and more elaborate programs as and when you become more proficient. Zorland C fits this description very well indeed.

One minor problem can arise for users of the Amstrad PC machines. Most other varieties of PC machine have a *linker* on the DOS disk. This is the program which links the object code produced by the compiler into a usable program, and no linker is supplied with the MS-DOS disk for the Amstrad machines. You therefore have to be sure that the compiler package that you buy contains a linker or provides this as an optional extra. As it happens, the lower-priced C compiler packages are excellent in this respect. Zorland formerly supplied the linker as an extra, but at the time of writing, the linker was being supplied as standard. This caused the disk set-up instructions in the Zorland manual to require correcting because the size of the linker means that the MS-DOS system cannot be contained on the main disk. Figure 2.2 shows an alternative disk arrangement which I have used.

One important point requires emphasis. If you are working with twin floppy disks, which is really the minimum requirement if you are using any kind of compiler, you are really equipped only for comparatively

Directory of A: disk

COMMAND	COM	23612	14–07–86	12:13
LINK	EXE	34160	12–06–87	11:02
ZC1	EXE	57776	28–04–87	21:55
ZC2	EXE	97936	28–04–87	21:51
ZC	COM	14053	2–07–87	11:05
CONFIG	SYS	128	13–02–87	14:17
GO	BAT	256	4–01–80	0:00
KEYBUK	EXE	2985	14–07–86	12:16
ZED	EXE	88272	10–06–87	14:09
	9 File(s)		37888 bytes free	

Directory of B: disk

C	OBJ	1594	23–01–87	1:56
STDIO	H	3301	13–01–87	18:14
NL	LIB	66560	24–03–87	16:00
ED	HLP	17941	10–06–87	14:01
MATH	H	1408	30–03–85	17:28
STRING	H	1067	19–07–86	16:37
	7 File(s)		247808 bytes free for programs	

Figure 2.2 The disk arrangement of the latest Zorland C for a machine using twin floppies.

short programs in C. By comparatively short, I mean the type of program like a utility or a small text editor; items which can be considerably longer than the examples in this book. For developing longer programs, you need to use the larger memory options in the compiler, and this in turn means that more disk space is needed. With floppies, this can involve a lot of swapping of disks in the course of compiling, and the use of a hard disk system is much to be preferred. At current prices of 20M and 30M disk cards, the saving in time will outweigh the money cost if you are really serious about C. This, however, is probably preaching to the converted because if you intend to learn C for professional purposes you are probably using a hard disk system already.

One final note concerns the type of program you get. The natural output from most compilers and linkers is a file with the .EXE extension. For some purposes, you may want to create .COM files which load faster and take up less of the memory. Your compiler may allow the direct generation of a .COM file; but the alternative is the conversion of an EXE file to COM using the EXE2BIN program which is included on the MS-DOS distribution disk. Once again, this need not concern you while you are learning C. Whatever your compiler provides is good enough to use while you are working with this book, and you can delve into the various options later.

3
The C Program

Starting simply

So far, you may have concluded that you now know a lot about the principles, but precious little about how you actually get your teeth into the C language. That's inevitable when you start to learn any structured language because until you know the reason why things are done the way they are, learning the language seems like a set of pointless rules and when you try to write programs for yourself you keep getting error messages whose purpose baffles you.

Error messages in most C compilers are not exactly what you are accustomed to in BASIC. Very often a compiler does not pick up an error at the point where the error exists, so that when your compiler stops with an error message the error may not be in the line that is displayed on the screen. Worse, still, the error message may not be particularly helpful in finding the error. Some compilers, and Zorland is one of them, are distinctly more helpful in this respect than others, but in general if you try to learn C in the way that you probably learned BASIC (write it, run it and see what happens) then you are in for a lot of frustration.

From what we have already looked at, then, the simplest possible outline of a C program is:

```
definitions
main()
{
statements;
}
```

and we now have to take a look at this in rather more detail. One point of detail that we need to look at is the C statement. In BASIC, a statement is an instruction like PRINT A which might be put into a (numbered) line or made part of a multistatement line and terminated with a colon. The end of a BASIC statement is therefore marked by the use of a new line or the use of a colon. In C, the end of a statement is marked by the use of a semicolon, and we have to be careful that the semicolon goes into the correct place. In BASIC, the semicolon is used to ensure that printing is to be kept on the same line, and the very different use of the semicolon in C takes some getting used to. In C, you can, for example, use the semicolon to separate statements in the same line, just as you use the colon in BASIC. Omitting the semicolon is a way of instructing the compiler that there is more of a statement to come, the kind of thing you might find in a test or a loop, for example.

Another point is that you can construct *compound statements*. These consist of a set of statements that start with an opening curly bracket and end with a closing curly bracket. A compound statement like this is treated as one single statement by the compiler, just as a multistatement line using colons is treated as a single line by the BASIC interpreter. At this stage, it's a bit pointless to describe the rules about semicolons in detail, because until you have had some experience in writing programs, you won't really see why semicolons are used in some places and not in others. For that reason, I'll point out in each of the early examples the few instances in which a semicolon has not been used where you might expect it.

In the example of program outline, the first line consists of the special name main (). A C program consists of a set of named functions, using whatever names you like to give them, but there must always be one that is called main (). The brackets are an essential part of this, and it's not very often that you need to put anything between these brackets. For other names of functions, though, you will want to place various items between the brackets. In any case, you can't omit them. The main () program is the one that calls up all of the other functions just as a BASIC core program can call up various subroutines. The curly brackets then show the start and the end of the main program, with the { indicating the start, and the } showing the end. You don't need any other way of marking the end of the program; the word END is not a reserved word of C and should not be used as such. When you want to read a C program, then, you look for main () and then read what is enclosed between the curly brackets. If the program is well laid out, taking one line for each statement and indenting lines that form part of a loop, the program should be very much clearer and easier to understand than a corresponding program in BASIC.

The way that a program is typed is of much more importance in C than it is in BASIC. One important point is the word *whitespace* (meaning spaces), the TAB character and the newline, all of which cause a blank space to appear on the screen. Whitespace characters are used in C as separators, and you cannot run words together in the casual way that so many varieties of BASIC allow. As you will see, some C functions are very fussy about whitespace characters, and this can be a source of problems unless you realise that, for example, one function might be arranged to skip over whitespace characters and another arranged specifically to look for them. When you use an INPUT in BASIC, you never stop to think that pressing the RETURN key adds another character to whatever you have typed, because BASIC is not organised in that way. In C, though, this is an important point because pressing the RETURN key adds a whitespace character, the newline at the end of whatever has been typed. Note that in C the newline character (ASCII 10) is the important one, the carriage return (ASCII 13) is incidental. Normal PC practice is to provide both when the RETURN key is pressed.

Indentation of lines in listings is also important, and it should conform to standards. The general rule is that groups of lines that belong together and form a sub-section of a function should be indented. For example, all of the lines that constitute a loop should be indented by at least one space and more usually one tab from the lines of the program that contains them, and if loops are nested then the indenting should be nested too. Indenting should make it easier to pick your way through a program listing, and it usually does, though if there are a lot of nested levels the appearance of the program can be unsatisfactory when lines have to be indented so far that the ends spill on to another line. In general, if you need that level of nesting and hence indenting your program is probably not very well constructed and will certainly run rather slowly.

As in BASIC, you can sprinkle comment/reminder lines about your program. This is very often omitted in a BASIC program because each REM in interpreted BASIC has to be read by the interpreter even if it is not going to be acted on. For a compiled C program, however, the reminder lines are only part of the source code, the ASCII text, and they don't exist in the object code (machine-code) which is the bit that actually runs. You can therefore afford to be quite generous with your reminders, subject to the amount of memory that will be needed for the text.

The reminder in C is marked with a combination of the forward slash and an asterisk, with no space between them. Unlike the REM of BASIC, you have to mark both the beginning and the end of each comment. At the start of the comment, you use / * and at the end you use * /, and you have to be careful to get the order correct. You also have to distinguish the forward slash / from the backslash \ because the backslash is used for very different purposes. A reminder, then, is written in the form:

/ *This is a reminder* /

and you would normally put it into a line by itself or following the end of a statement.

The simplest possible program is then written using keywords. A keyword in C is rather like a keyword in BASIC, it is reserved for a special

purpose and you can't use it for anything else. Keywords are always
typed in lower-case (small letters) and must be correctly spelled, otherwise an 'Undefined symbol' error will be announced during (or if you are
unlucky, after) compiling. This means that any of the errors which you
would think of as 'syntax errors' in BASIC are very often not discovered
in a C program until compiling time or even later. This wastes a lot of
time, so you need to be rather careful about checking what you type. An
important point here is that C always distinguishes between upper-case
(capitals) and lower-case letters, unlike some varieties of BASIC. Figure
3.1 shows the keywords of C which are used by all the major C compilers.

Words in bold print are not used in older versions of C

auto	break	case	char	**const**
continue	default	do	double	else
entry enum	extern	float	for	goto
	if	int	long	register
return	short	signed	sizeof	static
struct	switch	typedef	union	unsigned
	unsigned	**void**	**volatile**	while

Figure 3.1   The keywords of C. The list of C keywords always looks very
brief compared to the list of BASIC reserved words.

Note that some versions of C for specific machines will have a few
extra keywords, like the use of *inline* and *cast* in HiSoft C for the
Amstrad CP/M machines, and few compilers may get by with one or
two keywords less than this list but in general you will find that this list is
common to every compiler for the PC.

The word main, note, is not one of the keywords. This doesn't mean
that you can use it for anything you like, but it is a title for the main program, not a word which describes an action. This is an example of a word
which is an *identifier*. In BASIC, the only identifiers that you use are file-
names and names for variables. C uses a lot more types of identifiers,
and they are used in much more interesting ways. In this case, the word
'main' identifies the main program, and you could use other words to
identify the functions (the C replacement for subroutines) which are
called up by the main program. You also use identifiers for other things,
like variable names, subject to a few rules.

The rules are that an identifier must start with a letter, upper-case or
lower-case. Most compilers follow the normal C convention and treat
upper-case as being different from lower-case. Since you must use lower-
case for keywords, it makes sense to stick with lower-case for identifiers

too. Professional programmers use upper-case letters in identifiers which are present for special purposes, as we'll see later. You can then follow the first letter of an identifier with other letters or with digits, but no blanks or punctuation marks. The only character that is allowed, apart from letters and digits, is the underscore (_), which you get by pressing the SHIFT – key. The underscore is useful as a way of making long names more readable (like name_of_item). You could, if you wanted to, start a word with an underscore, but here again, it's better not to, because this could lead to trouble later on in your C programming career. The reason is that words which begin with an underscore are often used for special purposes to identify functions in the library, and unless you can be sure that you are using different words, you can cause problems. Zorland C typically allows you to use identifiers of 31 characters. You can use names of more than 31 characters, but only the first 31 characters will count; hardly a restriction. Remember, however, that disk file names are still subject to the rules of MS-DOS so that you can use only eight characters (the extension will often be fixed as .C for a source code and .OBJ for object code).

Some C compilers will contain a few built-in functions with identifier names which are already allocated. The more common approach, how-

Function	Action
atof	convert string to float
atoi	convert integer to float
calloc	allocate heap memory
fclose	close file
fgets	get string from file
fopen	open file
fprintf	print to file
fputs	put string to file
free	release heap memory
fscanf	input from file
getchar	get character from keyboard
gets	get string from keyboard
malloc	allocate heap memory
printf	print on screen
puts	print string to screen
scanf	read from keyboard

Figure 3.2 A few fundamental library functions that will be contained in any C library. You can expect to see a very much greater number in your own C library.

ever, is to provide all of these functions in the form of ready-compiled object code in a library. These functions are then included into your final program by the action of the linker. Each supplier of a C compiler package will have different ideas about what should be contained in a library, and the list in Fig. 3.2 is a selection of the most fundamental functions that you will almost certainly find in any C library. When you look at this list, you might think that there were another set of reserved words, as many of them would be in BASIC. The difference is important.

All of these identifier names can be used by you for something else if that's what you want. If, for example, you want to call your program gets or puts then you can do so. You would be foolish to do this, because by changing the meaning of these names, you are losing the use of some action that you might need, but you will not cause any error message. The difference is important, because if you try to use a reserved word for anything else, the error will be signalled; but if you use one of the 'predefined' identifier words, there's no error, and you won't be informed. You may wonder, however, why some action later turns out to be impossible!

Getting back to the program outline, following the main () identifier, there is a newline (obtained by pressing the RETURN or ENTER) key and the opening curly bracket which marks the beginning of any function. The next line will be the first statement of the program and it will end with a semicolon. You will normally take a new line following each semicolon in order to make the listing look neater. This isn't enforced upon you, and you can make the program one long chain of statements separated by semicolons if you want to, but if you can't read it afterwards it's your own fault.

Finally, the C program ends with the closing curly bracket. The pairs of curly brackets can be used in many places in a C program. This is because each section of a program has a beginning and an end, and the curly brackets are used to mark them. Any but the simplest C program will be written as a set of named functions that will be called by the main program, and each of these procedures will have an opening curly bracket and an ending curly bracket. If, incidentally, you miss out the opening curly bracket in the main program, you may find that the error is not picked up by the compiler as an omission of a curly bracket. The program will not compile, but the error message may not be about omitting a curly bracket. If you miss out the ending curly bracket you will get a message to the effect that there has been a premature end to the source file. Do not expect your compiler necessarily to report that a curly bracket is missing; some compilers do, others don't.

When we get to specific examples of programs, no matter how simple, it's important to try them out on your own compiler so as to get the feeling of the use of main () and the curly brackets. I know that the first few programs in any book on C look ridiculously simple, but you may very easily find that you can't produce a running program because there is something missing on one of your disks or because you have not set up the compiler in the way that the manufacturer recommended. Compiler packages are constantly being improved and updated for machine variations, and it's only too easy for a manual to get out of step with what is actually present on the disks. If you try some mistypings on these simple examples, you will see how your compiler deals with them. Find, for example, what type of error message you get when you miss out either kind of brackets or omit one of the terminators around a reminder line. Find out, also, at what stage you get the error message. With luck, all the errors will be picked up promptly by the compiler on the first pass and errors of this type will never make it to a later stage.

A few compilers can pick up some errors as you type them, and if you are using a C interpreter in place of a C compiler then you should have the same level of error reporting (or better) as you are accustomed to in BASIC. By exploring the error messages now you can save yourself a lot of trouble later because if you come across such messages in the course of working with a longer program it's comforting to know why the messages are being delivered. Without this experience you might be looking in the wrong places and assuming that what has gone wrong is very much more complicated than you think.

Storage classes

Once again, just as you are hoping to get your fingers on to the keys, there's something else to learn about. Once again, though, it's something that would cause a lot of bafflement and dismay if you met it with no warning, because there's nothing like it in BASIC. The subject is storage classes and it concerns the way in which your computer stores the value of variables. I should warn you at this point that some of this topic betrays the fact that C was designed before microcomputers existed so that some storage classes simply don't exist on micros.

To start with, you don't normally have to think how variables are stored in a BASIC program. When a BASIC program runs, its variables are stored in the memory which lies just beyond the program text area. As each new variable appears in the program, a new space is created so that this storage is dynamic, changing all the time. This also explains why most BASIC interpreters cannot allow you to continue with running a program after making changes. The changes that you have made will have altered the length of the program listing and altered items in the memory where the variables are stored. After editing then, you have to run your BASIC program from scratch so as to build up the variable values in the memory again.

C appears to offer you more choice by permitting various classes of variable storage. To some extent, this is an illusion, because the storage will normally be in the memory and the main difference is how long it is held there. In a very complete version of C for a mainframe machine you might find classes labelled as *auto*, *static*, *extern* and *register*. The register class will be absent on microcomputers. As the name suggests, this allocates a register of the processor for each variable and none of the microprocessors that are used in small computers are ever equipped with enough registers to allow this. The register class was devised to allow for very fast access to some variables in mainframe computers. Zorland C, like most compilers will change any register class into auto. The important storage classes for our purposes are therefore auto, static and extern.

The most important storage class is auto, and it is a default in the sense that if you do not specify a storage class, auto is what you get. An automatic variable is one that is local inside the function in which it is defined. If you define an auto variable filnam in a function called spotit, then this variable exists only between the start and the end of the function spotit. If spotit calls in turn another function spillit, then the variable filnam can be passed to this function, and it can be used also in spotit after spillit has ended. When function spotit ends, however, variable filnam no longer exists, and has no value. Since at least 95% of the variables that you use need to be local like this, it makes sense to have auto as the default. These auto variables are stored on the stack, the part of memory that is allocated for temporary storage.

The static class of variable is an interesting compromise between a local and a global one. Suppose you have a function that defines and uses the name count. At the start of the function, the value of count is initialised to zero, and somewhere else in the function, count is incremented. When the function runs for the first time, then, count is assigned with the value 0 and then this is later incremented to 1. When the function returns to main, or to whatever function called it, there is no longer a variable called count. The next time the function is called the process will simply repeat. If this variable is static, however, the value it ended up with the first time round is stored in a more permanent area of memory. The next time the function is called, the initialising step will be ignored and count starts with a value of 1, ready to be incremented to 2. On the next call of the same function, the value of count will be incremented to 3 and so on.

Static variables retain their values after a function that contains them has ended, even though the name of the variable is deleted and might be used by another variable in the program. The use of static variables is handy if you want to keep track of how many times a function has been called, or keep track of which elements of an array are being used. In addition, some actions require the use of static variables.

If you want to declare and initialise an array in one step, for example, the array variable must be declared as a static one. The best course is to use static variables only when you really need them, which is when you have to keep a value preserved between one call to a function and the next, or when an array is provided with values at the time when it is declared. If you follow this advice, you will seldom use statics, and that's a sensible course to follow.

The other class of storage is external, abbreviated to extern. This is a variable which has been declared somewhere else, in another program file, for example. Once again, the requirement for using an extern variable is quite rare, particularly when you are learning to use C for the first time, and auto is your default first choice.

The pre-processor

One feature of any C compiler is very much like a word-processor action, and is certainly not like the action of anything in BASIC. This is, for historical reasons, called the pre-processor, because all the actions in this section of a program have to be carried out before compiling can start. The action is of the search and replace type, and one common type of line in this section begins with the word #define. A line that starts with #define is used to define something that will be used as a constant in the program. We have already met the idea that the letters EOF might be defined to mean the number (usually − 1) that is used to indicate the end of a file. This would be put in by the line:

#define EOF − 1

putting a gap between each of the three parts of the definition. Anything that might be used as a constant in a program should be defined before the start of main in this way, and common items for such definitions are CR for ASCII 13, TAB for ASCII 9, BS for ASCII 8 and so on. The search and replace action of the pre-processor will then replace each set of these letters in the program by the number that it is defined to represent.

Even more usefully, you can define strings in this way, allowing you to produce messages in the program. For example, using:

#define ERMES "Warning − error"

will allow you to produce the full error message by printing ERMES. This use of #define is not the same as assigning a variable, because the item that is defined in this way is put into full form into the program listing in each place where it is used.

To make this clearer, suppose you had a static string variable which was assigned as TXT. Now since this is a static variable, it will be stored in some part of the memory and when TXT is printed, the print routine obtains the memory address for the text and prints it, but only this one copy is held in the memory. If, however, you had used a define line such as:

#define TXT "This is a message"

then wherever you use TXT in the program, the pre-processor action would put in the letters of the message in ASCII code before the compiling process started.

The difference between variables and these defined constants is rather like the difference between subroutines and macros if you have met macros in your use of the PC. The #define lines are macros, pieces of text with abbreviations, and the action of the pre-processor is to work on the text so as to expand each abbreviation out into its full text, like the search and replace action of a word-processor. Your compiler may allow the #define lines to specify actions as well as constants, so that you can have lines such as:

#define SUMSQ(a,b) sqr(a*a + b*b)

which can be used in the program to get the square root of the sum of squares of two number variables. Not all compilers will accept this unorthodox type of syntax, and you will need to check how your own compiler deals with such lines. At the very least, you will probably need have the line #include < math.h > along with your #define line, and even then, you may find that the action does not work on most compilers. It's very important not to have a space between the name of the defined word and any brackets that follow it, because a space is taken as the marker between the name and the item that is to be substituted for the name. It is also very important not to end such a #define line with a semicolon, because this would make the semicolon part of the substituted text.

The reason for the name of *pre-processor* is that in early C compilers for mainframes a separate program was needed to process all the #define lines before the program could be compiled. This separate program was the pre-processor, the part that filled in the definitions so saving time in compiling. Nowadays, most compilers include this acton and there is no separate pre-processor section though there must be a routine that carries out the substitutions in the text before the compiler can get to work.

One of the most common pre-processor actions apart from #define is #include. This allows the contents of another file to be included in the compilation, and is often found at the start of a program in order to allow a file of standard #define lines to be added; it can also be used to join source-code programs before compiling. When you use the same set

fclose	feof	ferror	fflush
fgetc	fgets	fopen	fputc
fputs	fread	freopen	fseek
ftell	fwrite	getc	getch
getche	getchar	max	min
putc	putchar		

Figure 3.3   The use of #include < stdio.h > in Zorland D is required for these functions.

of #define lines in every one of your programs, this is a very useful way of ensuring that they all get into place each time. In addition, compilers make use of #include to gain access to a standard library of functions. For example, if your program contains some types of input or output routines, then you will have to use as your first line:

#include < stdio.h >

in order to include automatically the stdio.h file of input/output routines from the library. You have to learn for yourself when this type of #include will be needed; and Fig. 3.3 shows when it has to be used in Zorland C, which follows standard C practice in requiring the name of the file to be enclosed in angle brackets, <>. Figure 3.4 shows the other .h files of Zorland C which needed to be specified by a #include line for various purposes. Though a lot of programs can be created using only the < stdio.h > files, it's often useful to have the < math.h > and < string.h > files stored in the same disk or directory, and for more specialised work you might want to keep all of the .h files handy.

Other definition lines starting with the hash sign include #if, #endif, #elif, #ifdef, #ifndef, #line and #undef. To undo the effect of a #define you use #undef, and the others are used as instructions to the compiler to check the contents of the pre-processor section. At this level we can ignore them all. Your compiler may use a few # expressions for specialised purposes, and these will be features of that compiler rather than of the C language. For example, Zoland uses #message to write a message during compilation and #exit to abort a compilation (following a #if test) for some problem, like trying to compile a program that contains floating-point numbers with the integer version of the compiler.

assert.h	ctype.h	disp.h	dos.h
errno.h	math.h	msmouse.h	setjmp.h
time.h			

Figure 3.4   The other .h files of Zorland C. Other compilers will not necessarily use the same list.

4
Practical Fundamentals

It is time now to start some practical programming. If you feel that it isn't one moment too soon, then I sympathise, but you'll see when you get further into C for yourself why I took so long to get to this point. Even now we're not exactly going to plunge into any very fancy programming. The main thing at this point is to establish how we carry out some fundamental actions in C, because unless you can write program lines for such elementary things as printing to the screen and the input of values into a program, you are not going to get very far with C. Some textbooks are notably bad in this respect; they plunge you right in and expect you to cope. Softly, softly is the watchword here. It's fine to dive in if you are in company with an instructor to hand. If you are struggling along with your own machine and relying entirely on a book to learn from, then the slower the better. In any case, what follows is going to require you to know how to use the compiler, and you should have it loaded and ready.

Output to the screen

You have probably already noticed that C does not have a reserved word print. There is, in fact, no reserved word for the action of putting something on the screen. This action is one which carries an identifier name for a library function routine rather then being one of the reserved name actions. The identifier word that you need is printf, and the routine will normally be read from your library and linked into your program. No #include < stdio > line is needed in order to work with printf. The use of printf is, however, quite different from the use of PRINT in BASIC. The name printf has to be followed in brackets with details of what has to be printed. This means not only what you want to print, but also how you want it printed, formatting as it's called. The action of printf corresponds more closely to PRINTUSING in BASIC than to PRINT.

   The formatting commands and the items that you want to print are all included within brackets, with quotes around the formatting commands and any characters that are to be printed as a message apart from

```
main()
{
 printf("\n My message");
 printf("\n%d",5+3*2);
}
```

Figure 4.1 A short program in 'C' to get you familiar with compiling. This uses printf to place words and numbers on the screen.

variables. In some cases, you will use printf only with direct messages placed between quotes inside the brackets, and no formatting commands. You can place a formatting command within the brackets and follow it by a comma, then the number or string variable you want to print. What is 'written' on the screen in this way can be a number or it can be text. The simplest possible examples of text writing look sufficiently like BASIC to be easily understood when you are reading a C program. Figure 4.1 shows an example, which you can type, compile and run.

In this example, the actions are of writing a word and performing a piece of arithmetic. The writing of a word is rather different to the PRINT "Words" that would be used in BASIC. The word has to be placed between quotes, and also has to be placed between brackets. The semicolon at the end of the line has nothing to do with the printing action, remember, it's just the signal to the compiler that there is more to come.

The real novelty here is the \n which appears within the quotes and just ahead my My message. The \is the backslash sign, which is on the key next to the left-hand SHIFT key. Don't mix this up with the forward

Mark	Meaning
\0	NULL
\t	Tab
\n	newline
\r	return
\f	form feed
\b	backspace
\\	backslash
\'	apostrophe
\123	octal number 123
\x1F	hex number 1F

Figure 4.2 The specifier letters which can follow the backslash in a printf statement.

slash next to the right-hand shift key which is used in /∗rem∗/ lines.
The effect of \n coming before the text is to force a newline before anything is printed. You could also place another \n after the text to cause a
new line to be taken after printing. There is a complete set of these backslash instructions, all of which must be included between quotes in a
printf type of statement. Figure 4.2 shows this set. If, for example, you
use \f this will carry out a formfeed if sent to the printer, but places
a ♀ symbol on the screen. Note that in this particular line, the quotes
enclose both the formatting instruction \n and the text 'My message'.
This is not the way that printf is used along with variable names or with
arithmetic instructions.

In the next line, the formatting characters are still placed between
quotes, but the numbers are not. The arithmetic result is printed out, just
as it would be by PRINT 5 + 3∗2 in BASIC. As in BASIC, the multiplication is carried out before the addition, so that the result is 11, not 16.
Here again a semicolon has been used to mark the end of the statement
and there's another \n used to cause a newline. The novelty this time is
the %d which follows the \n. The % sign is a general way of indicating
how you would like an item of data printed, and when it's followed by a
d, then the number is an integer printed in *denary*. If you haven't come
across this term before, it means the ordinary scale-of-ten numbers that
we use. Once again, there is a whole set of these 'specifiers', and Fig. 4.3

Mark	Meaning
%d, %i	Signed denary number, range −32768 to +32767.
%u	Unsigned denary number, range 0 to 65535.
%o	Unsigned octal number.
%x, %X	Unsigned hexadecimal number (x = lower-case, X = upper-case).
%c	Single character.
%s	String ending with a zero.
%g, %G	Double with e or E format.
%e, %E	Double in scientific format.
%f	Double, ordinary notation.
%%	Print % sign.

Quantities are normally printed right justified, but using a negative sign
before the specifier letter will force left justification. Each specifier letter can
be preceded by a number to set minimum field size, 0 will print a leading zero
or blank. See your compiler manual for details of the formatting of floats and
doubles.

Figure 4.3 The formatting code letters which can follow the % sign in a
printf statement.

shows the complete list. After this line, the main program ends with the curly bracket.

This very simple program nevertheless illustrates a lot of important points about C. The most important point is that the program consists entirely of calls to functions. There is absolutely no processing in the main program, simply two calls to the printf function. The brackets, which we did not use in main () are used in printf to carry the items that we want to print, and also the instruction codes about how we want it all printed, with a comma separating the formatting instructions from the item(s) except when a phrase is being printed. This is the way of carrying out most actions in C, and very often we have to write our own functions if there is nothing suitable in the library.

Now after typing this program and saving the text under a suitable file-name, compile and link the program. It is important to record the file, because the C compiler will normally work from the recorded version on disk, and if you are using the Zorland compiler you will then press the 'O' key twice, and then RETURN, to start the automatic process of compiling and linking. The RETURN key may have to be pressed once more after the first run through the compiler (ZC1), and when linking is complete, pressing RETURN once more will run the program, assuming that all has gone well.

You will find now that your data disk contains three files. One will be your text file, and the normal convention is that such a file should use the .C extension, so you might have filed it as TEST.C. This file is called the 'source-code'. Until this source code has been compiled it is just a file of ASCII codes, nothing more. Once compiled, it is object code, closer to machine-code and quite different in action, and with the .OBJ extension, so that if you used TEST.C for the source code, the object file will be TEST.OBJ. The most important difference from your point of view is that the source code can be read, edited, and is easily understood. The object code has no meaning unless you know about machine-code, is very difficult to edit, and is really only an intermediate step unless you intend to place it into the library, which is something that we are not ready for yet. The final version of this file is TEST.EXE which will also be on the disk. This is the file which can from now on be run by typing TEST. Some compilers allow you the option of compiling either to an EXE file or a COM file, but for the purposes of this book the difference is not important. Once again, when you have this program up and running it's a good idea to experiment with a few deliberate errors so that you can see what error messages you get from your compiler. Using the Zorland compiler, most errors of this type will be noted on the first pass through the compiler so that you don't have to wait long to find what happens.

Using a variable

When you use a constant, like. 3.1416, in BASIC, you are always advised
to assign the value to a variable name. The reason is that this avoids the
requirement for the BASIC interpreter to change from the ASCII codes
into number form each time the number is used. C does not suffer from
this problem, because, as we shall see, such a number can be defined as a
constant by making use of a #define line. True variables are quantities
that will be changed in the course of a program, and to start with we shall
look at the use of integer variables, because a surprising variety of programs can be written that use only integer numbers.

The integer declaration uses the reserved name int. As we saw in
Chapter 2, you can declare that a name will be used for an integer and
then assign a number to this name. The syntax of declaration is:

    int quadro;

using the reserved word int followed by a space and then the identifier
name quadro. The position of this declaration line, following the first
curly bracket of main makes this variable local to main, and you have to
be careful, as we'll see later over the positioning of declaration lines like
this. One useful rule for the moment is that you would not normally have
a declaration line between main () and the opening curly bracket. You
can have several such declarations on the same line, with commas following each name. For example, you could have a line:

    int duo,tri,quad;

if you wanted to declare several names as integers. Note the semicolon to
show the end of the statement, which is the end of that declaration. Once
the names have been declared, you can make assignments to these
names, using integer numbers. Figure 4.4 shows a simple program which
makes use of the integer quin to mean 5. In this example, the declaration
of the integer and its assignment are both straightforward but the printf
line is not. In C, printing is a very different kind of operation as compared to BASIC, because of the formatting characters.

```
main()
{
 int quin; /* declare integer */
 quin=5; /* assignment */
 printf("\n%d times 3 is %d",quin,quin*3);
}
```

Figure 4.4 An example of declaration, assignment, calculation and formatted printing.

The first part of the printf statement consists of the words and formatting instructions only. We want two numbers to be printed, both in denary form. In the phrase that is to be used, then, the %d is put into each part where a number will be printed in the version we see on the screen. Once the quotes are closed, the numbers variable names are put in, using the same left to right order, and with commas used to separate the numbers. The numbers are quin and quin∗3, the result of a calculation. Once again, this printf line is a statement and it has to end with a semicolon. When it prints on the screen, you see the message:

   5 times 3 is 15

which is not exactly world-shaking but until you get used to the way in which C uses its printf statement, it's an example that you will probably want to consult now and again.

Constants

The use of a variable for holding a number in C is close enough to the methods of BASIC (so far) to cause you little worry. There is an alternative in C, however, for storing items which you might want to use in any part of a program. These items are called, logically enough, *constants*, and they have to be defined in a way that is quite different from our definition of variables. The definition of a constant is done at the beginning of a program, before the main() portion or (almost) anything else. The syntax is simple enough, #define, followed by a space and then the name that you want to use, another space and the value. There must be no semicolon at the end of a #define line. Constants can be numbers, single characters or strings, as you please, providing you assign correctly and use correctly. Take a look, for example, at Fig. 4.5.

The line which 'declares the constant' of mile is situated immediately at the start of the program, using #define mile 1760. In the main program, the part which lies between the curly brackets, we will use mile as meaning the number 1760, the number of yards in a mile (remember

```
#define mile 1760  /* declare a constant */
main()
{
 int ml;  /* declare integer */
 ml=3;  /* assign integer */
 printf("\n%d miles is %d yards",ml,ml*mile);
 /* uses constant as multiplier */
}
```

Figure 4.5 Using #define to place a constant into a program.

them?). This meaning must be declared before the program begins. This way, the compiler has allocated memory space for the constant and is ready to use it before the program needs it.

As we have seen, you might have to allocate several constants like this before a program starts. These constants need not all be integer numbers like 1760. They could be letters or phrases, like 'Press any key', and this use of a constant replaces a lot of the purposes for which we use string variables in BASIC. This is important, because C does not have string variables in the form that we use in BASIC. One point you have to look for is the use of *long* constants, meaning numbers which are larger than the integer range. The rule is that these numbers should be ended with a letter L (a lower-case 'l' is acceptable, but much too easily confused with number one). For example, the line:

    #define mega 1000000L

defines mega as meaning one million, and the L marks this number out as a long integer, so that the compiler will deal with it correctly (not treating it as a float, for example).

In the example, you can see the printf phrase "\n%d miles is %d yards" used with the %d to specify where the numbers will be printed, as denary numbers. Following the phrase comes the quantities, the integer variable ml and the constant mile. In this example, the numbers have been printed as denary numbers, but can force any printf action to produce numbers in other forms, such as hex or octal, that you want. You can also decide how much space you want the number to take up. Try a change to the printf line, so that it reads:

    printf("\n% – 6d miles is %8d yards",ml,ml*mile);

and compile and run this one. You will see that the figure '3' appears on the left-hand side of the screen, and the number 5280 is spaced out from the word 'is', taking up eight character positions. As you may have guessed, the figure 8 along with the 'd' specifies that the number shall be printed taking up eight character positions, and placed at the right-hand side (right-justified). By using a minus sign in front of the number, the space is allocated similarly, but the number is set over to the left (left-justified).

This type of control over number position is called *fielding*, and it's much easier in C than it is in BASIC. If you don't use any numbers along with the 'd' in formatting, a number will simply take up whatever space it needs in the printf statement. You can, of course, decide on the number of spaces either ahead of or following the number by putting them in with the spacebar. The fielding method is particularly useful if you want numbers organised in columns, and really comes into its own when floating point numbers with decimal fractions are being used because it allows the decimal point to be lined up, something that can be quite troublesome in BASIC.

I said that a constant did not have to be a number, but could be a character or a string. For items like that, you still use #define, with the name that you want to allocate, and the character or string spaced from it. The character or string needs to be surrounded by quotes, as Fig. 4.6 shows. If you omit the quotes you will get an error message during compiling when the character or string is used, rather than where it is defined. The message will be 'undefined variable', but if you surround the characters with marks other than quotes you can get some quite exotic error messages. The other part of the deal is that if you want to print messages in this way, the printf statement needs to be changed. In place of the %d that you needed to specify an integer number in denary form, you need to use %s for a string or %c for a single character. Without these modifiers, *nothing* gets printed!

```
#define mesg "press any key"
#define key "Y"
/* string constants */
main()
{
 printf("\n use the %s key or ",key);
 printf("\n%s",mesg);
}
```

Figure 4.6 Using #define for string or character constants.

In the example, %s has been used for both, but we could have used %c for the single character. The use of #define in this way allows a lot more than just the occasional number constant or message phrase. With #define, you can make your programs much more readable, particularly by definitions such as #define white 0 and #define black 1, which allow you to use words in place of numbers for items such as board games, or allocate values to items, as in #define Mayfair "£5000".

More variables

We have already made use of an integer variable in a program, and the style is easy enough. There's much more to this type of variable than meets the eye, however. A variable which is declared as, for example, int num is what is called an *automatic* variable. In all varieties of C, you can state this by typing auto int num, but if you don't use any word before int, then the use of auto is assumed, it's the default. Most of the variables that you are likely to use in programs will be auto types, simply because of convenience. We have noted in Chapter 3 that you would probably want to use auto variables for most purposes, but there are exceptions in some compilers in which the use of static variables considerably speeds up program execution at the expense of storage space. You might, for example, want to make use of static variables in games programs so as to get the highest possible speed of access to data.

One feature of C variables that can be useful is declaration and initialisation in one step. The way that you can declare and assign in one operation in BASIC, such as A% = 5, is very useful and the very brief example in Fig. 4.7 the same type of action in C. This declares an int and in the same line makes the assignment of 8 for its value. The printf statement then shows that the assignment has been carried out. Combined declaration and assignment for single variables such as char, integer and float is uncomplicated, but you have to be more careful about such steps when you are working with arrays, as we shall see later.

```
main()
{
 int squares=8;
 /* declaration and assignment */
 printf("\n%d",squares);
}
```

Figure 4.7 Simultaneous declaration and assignment of an integer.

Getting a value

Suppose that we extend the use of an integer variable to a variable whose value is entered from the keyboard? One of the standard identifier words for reading an input is getchar(), which is a function that requires the use of the stdio.h header. In other words, we can't use the getchar() function from the library unless we have the line:

#include < stdio.h >

at the start of the program, before any functions are defined. One of the things that makes C seem very awkward to the former BASIC programmer is the lack of anything like the BASIC INPUT statement. Instead, you have to use library functions that are matched to the kind of data that you want to read, and some of them require stdio.h, others don't. As far as getchar() is concerned, this is used to read a single character, and it requires the use of stdio.h. If you forget the use of stdio.h in this example you will get the error message 'unsatisfied getchar' after compiling and linking, so it's important to make sure that these #include lines are correctly put in.

Using this built-in function, however, brings us up against one of the features that newcomers to C find irritating – the use of characters. The function getchar() will get characters from the keyboard, meaning that you can type any character, digit or letter, that you like. If you look up the action of this function in the compiler manual, however, you see it described as int getchar(), meaning that it gives you (or returns) an integer. Whatever you type at this point is accepted as an ASCII code, and this is the integer value that you get. What we are going to type is a number which will have to be assigned to a variable name of x. The value of x, however, will be an ASCII code. For the numbers 1 to 9, this means a code in the range 49 to 57. We can get the number values back from this by subtracting 48, the value of ASCII '0'. Now we can do this in two ways. One way would be the familiar BASIC way, as x = x − 48. We can however, also write it as: x = x − '0', meaning that we subtract the ASCII code for zero. This second form is a lot easier to use and understand – for one thing, you don't have to strain your memory for the ASCII codes! This is the method that is illustrated in Fig. 4.8.

```
#include <stdio.h>
/* needed for using getchar() */
main()
{
 int x;
 printf("Please type a number, 0 to 9 \n");
 x=getchar();   /* get from keyboard */
 x=x-'0';   /* convert from ASCII */
 printf("\n Double this is %d",2*x);
}
```

Figure 4.8 Using a function to obtain a keyboard ASCII code for a digit, and converting to number form.

Using getchar(), as you'll gather, is rather primitive. Though you can type more than one digit, the function works only on the first, which is why the program limits input to the range 1 to 9. There is a function called atoi() in the library for converting characters into numbers, but that's for later. There is also, in the library, a routine which corresponds more closely to BASIC's INPUT, but without the facility to mix questions and input like INPUT "Answer: ";a$ in BASIC. The trouble with using these routines right at the start of your conversion to C is that they involve a lot of new ideas, and we can't ever take in too much at one time.

Other variable types

By the time any book on BASIC has reached this stage, the subject of string variables would have appeared. Now strings have an important part to play in C, as they have in any language, but the way that strings are handled is not quite so simple if you are making a transition from BASIC to C. The reason is that STRING is not a pre-defined variable type, it isn't in the list of ready-made identifiers of Fig. 3.2. We've looked already at how we can use a string in a # define line, and when you think about the way you use strings, this probably takes care of more than 60% of the need for strings in most of your programs. Later, we'll look at how this type of identifier can be created but for the moment we'll look at the characters that make up a string.

C, in common with several other languages, has a variable type called char which, as we have seen means any character of the computer which is represented by an ASCII code. In compilers for the PC machines, this could include the graphics character as well as the ordinary alphabetical and digit characters, and you can try the response of getchar() to the usual PC dodge of holding down the Alt key and then typing an ASCII code. Now with this char variable, we can do the actions that you associate with PRINT CHR$() in BASIC, and then some more. Take a look at Fig. 4.9, for example. The #include line has been used with

```
#include <stdio.h>
/* needed for using putchar() */
main()
{
 char m1,m2,m3;
 m1=65;m2=66;m3=167;
 system("cls");/* Zorland clear screen */
 putchar('\n');
 putchar(m1);
 putchar(m2);
 putchar(m3);
}
```

Figure 4.9 Using the equivalent of BASIC CHR$.

< stdio.h > because putchar is being used. Three char types are defined, variables m1, m2 and m3. These are assigned with ASCII codes 65, 66 and 167, to illustrate the use of putchar. The routine that clears the screen is a Zorland one, the system function that allows you to insert any MS-DOS command (held between brackets and double quotes) into a program. In this case, using system ("cls") will have the MS-DOS CLS

action of clearing the screen. If you are using a different compiler you will have to consult the manual to find what you can use here. The use of char means that the variable consists of one ASCII code, stored in one byte of memory. The putchar(c) routine is called from the library, and it prints one character – this is another function that requires the use of stdio.h. This function requires the argument (value to print) which is shown as c in the manual description for the library function, but we can substitute any name of type char that we like. In this example, the substitution is of m1, m2 and m3 in succession, so printing the values assigned to these variables. Note from the m3 example that you can print the graphics and special symbols as well as the normal ASCII range of 32 to 127.

5
Data Types Again

Before we get involved with arithmetic operators, we must do some
memory refreshing on data types. The main primary data types are
integer (*short*, *long* and/or *unsigned*), *float* (*ordinary* or *double*) and
character. All of these make use of number variables, because a
character is just an ASCII code number. Of the simpler types, a
character can be stored in one byte, a short integer or short unsigned in
two bytes, and a long integer or unsigned in four bytes. An ordinary float
makes use of four bytes, and a double uses eight. When any arithmetic is
carried out with floats, however, each float is converted to double form
so as not to lose precision in the operation. If your PC contains the 8087
number-cruncher chip, then it should be possible to use this chip for all
floating-point calculations, greatly speeding these up. The Zorland compiler will automatically use the 8087 if one is installed.

The use of four bytes for an ordinary number allows floats to take
values ranging from -1.701411^{38} to $+1.701411^{38}$, but with a precision of
only around six places of decimals. This is not really enough, even if you
are dealing with financial programs that work to the nearest penny,
because the errors in storing ordinary floats will accumulate until the
difference becomes noticeable. The use of double-precision allows much
greater precision, to about twelve places of decimals, but at the cost of
more storage space and slower handling unless the 8087 is present. This is
why the compiler carries out all floating point arithmetic with doubles,
even if the answer is an ordinary float. You need to watch this point
because any float constants that you define with #define will normally
be treated as doubles by the compiler, and you will probably have to use
#include < math.h >.

Given then that all of the primary data types of C are number types,
what happens if you mix them. You would hardly think of adding a
character to an intger, but C is not fussy, and this has given C rather a
bad name among more academic programmers, otherwise known as the
Cosa Pascal. In C arithmetic, mixing data types causes the automatic
conversion of types until an answer can be obtained.

The first conversions are from char (or short) to integer, and from ordinary float to double. What happens after that depends on what arithmetic is to be performed. For example, if the expression contains a double after the first conversions, then all other numbers are converted to this form and the answer is also of this form. If the longest form of number is an integer, then the answer will be an integer. The important point is that these conversions are automatic, and they are also performed by several varieties of BASIC that permit the use of double-precision numbers (such as BASICA and GW BASIC). The type that you have to get used to is the char, because in BASIC you don't normally think of characters as being single-byte numbers, though if you have programmed in assembly language the idea will be quite natural.

Some operations

There aren't many programs that you are likely to write that don't involve the operators of C. The operators are the symbols which control actions on numbers, including characters, and C is rather richer in operators than BASIC. In addition, some of the actions and the order in which they are carried out need rather more thought than you would give to similar things in BASIC. Several operators relate to items (such as pointers) that we haven't met so far, and we'll concentrate for the moment only on operators that will be reasonably familiar.

The four main operators of $*/+-$ are specified just as they are in BASIC, and the only thing to look out for is the effect of division if you happen to be using a compiler that is restricted to integers only. You can, however, use the % operator to find a remainder (or *modulus*). The expression z%x, for example, means 'find the remainder after z has been divided by x'. This quantity must be an integer, and the numbers stored as z and as x must also be integers. If you are using an integer-only compiler, or if you are using your compiler in integer mode, then the use of the / and % operators allows you to carry out divisions and show the result as a quotient and remainder. Using a floating-point compiler with the / operator would allow the number to be displayed as a quotient that included a decimal fraction.

Operator classes

The simple arithmetic operators $+-*/$ and % are all classed as *binary operators*, meaning that each one of them requires two numbers to act on. Don't be confused by the term binary in this sense, it doesn't mean that you have to write everything in binary coded numbers. The classification of operators generally is as *unary* (one number needed), *binary* (two numbers) and *ternary* (three numbers). At this point, then, it looks like a good idea to list just what operators are available in these different classes. Figure 5.1 shows the list of the main unary operator symbols, some of which will not be discussed in detail until later.

Operator	Action
*	pointer to variable
&	address of variable
−	negate (make negative)
!	change 0 to 1 and 1 to 0
~	one's complement
++	Increment variable value.
− −	Decrement variable value.

Figure 5.1 The main unary operators of C.

The first two operators, * and &, are in this class because they can carry out unary actions on pointers, and as such we defer discussion of them until Chapter 7. The − sign used as a unary operator simply changes the sign of the number it affects. This action is sometimes called the negate action. The ! sign is a form of two-value negate. If you have an expression !x, then the effect of the ! sign will be to make the result either 0 or 1, the opposite of the existing value. For example, if x is 1, then !x is 0, and if x is 0, then !x is 1. This can be a very useful operator for testing values of this kind. The ~ operator gives a result that is the one's complement of a binary-code number. This is a rather more specialised action unless you are used to working with binary codes, and if you are unfamiliar with one's complement then consult Appendix A.

The effects of these unary operators, along with the ++ and − − types, are illustrated in Fig. 5.2, which lets you see them in action on your own screen. The ! effect is straightforward, and Fig. 5.3 explains the effect of the ~ operator on the integer numbers 15 and − 20. The next line

```
main()
{
int x,y,w;
x=1;y=0;
printf("\n !x is %d, !y is %d",!x,!y);
x=15;y=-20;
printf("\n ~x is %d ~y is %d",~x,~y);
x=3;
w=++x;y=x++;
printf("\n w is %d, y is %d and x is %d",w,y,x);
}
```

Figure 5.2 A program that illustrates the effects of some unary operators.

The number 15 in two-byte binary code is:
0000 0000 0000 1111   (groups of four only for easy reading)
and the ~ operator converts this into:
1111 1111 1111 0000
In unsigned denary, this is 65520, in signed denary it is −16

The number −20 in two-byte binary code is:
1111 1111 1110 1100
and the ~ operator converts this into:
0000 0000 0001 0011
In denary, signed or unsigned, this is +19.

Figure 5.3   The effect of the ~ operator on the numbers 15 and −20.

of the program carries out an action which is quite certainly unfamiliar in BASIC. The assignment w = + + x means that the value of variable x is incremented and then assigned to variable w. The next part of the line then assigns the value of x to y, and then increments this value of x again. The printed values of w, y and x then show what has been done. The effect of the + + sign is to increment the value of a variable, and the effect of − − (not illustrated here) is to decrement the value of a variable.

Just as important as the action itself, however, is the timing of the actions, and this is why the position of the symbols is important. The printout states that w is 4, y is 4 and x is 5. Using the increment sign + + following the variable name means that the increment action has been carried out following the assignment, not before. If you make the line read:

   w=x++;y=++x;

then the result is 'w is 3 and y is 5' because w = x + + made w equal to 3 and then x equal to 4, while y = + + x made x equal to 5 and then carried out an assignment of the same value to y. The use of increment and decrement can be very useful in loops, as we shall see, but you have to think out the order of things carefully. This becomes more difficult when you get to complicated expressions, so it's advisable to start with the easy ones.

Note that there is no square root among these unary operators. The square root function sqrt is one of your library functions, and you will have to remember to use the floating-point version of your compiler (the default for Zorland C) and to have the #include < maths.h > line at the start of the program listing.

Operator	Action
*	Multiply quantities.
/	Divide, yield quotient.
%	Modulus, remainder of integer division.
+	Add quantities.
−	Subtract quantities.
<	Less than.
>	Greater than.
<=	Less than or equal to.
>=	Greater than or equal to.
==	Identical to.
!=	Not equal to.
&&	AND action.
||	OR action.
=	Assign value.

Note: There is also one ternary operator, which is:

?:   Select one or other.

Figure 5.4   The binary operators of C, meaning the operators that require two numbers to work on.

Binary operators

The binary operators are the ones that need two numbers to work on, and they are listed in Fig. 5.4. Of these, the ordinary arithmetic symbols of * / % + and − have been mentioned already. The signs ≫ and ≪ cause binary-code bit shifting, and along with & (bit AND), ˆ (bit XOR) and |(bit OR) have been consigned to Appendix B. The remaining operators may look more familiar, but you should not assume that they will work in a familiar way. For example, the comparisons <, >, <= and >= make the usual comparisons of less than, more than, less or equal and more or equal, but the result of such comparisons is always 0 or 1, meaning false or true. The == sign means identical to, and the != sign means not equal, and the really hard thing for the BASIC-reared programmer to remember is that the meanings of == and of = must be distinguished. To assign a quantity, = is used, to test for identity, == is used. BASIC uses a single equality sign for both purposes, something that is done by no other high level language, and a considerable stumbling block when you have been reared on BASIC. The confusion can be so great that the Zorland compiler asks you to double check any line in which the symbols might have been mistaken. A common culprit is if(a = b) instead of if(a == b). The first version will assign the value of b to a, and test for this being zero or not. The second one gives a true answer only if a is identical to b, and this is usually what is required.

The logical operators

The logical operators in BASIC are the words AND and OR that are used to connect two conditions. The problems with their use in BASIC is that they are sometimes used for a rather different purpose also, bitwise operations, so that when you use AND and OR in BASIC you have to know the syntax of that particular BASIC very well in order to be absolutely certain what the use of these operators will give you. In C, these two are represented by symbols, and we use && for AND and || for OR. These two relational operators are used in lines such as:

    if(n&&a)printit;

which also illustrated how concise C can be about these things. Translated, it means that if the variables n and a are both non-zero, then function printit will run. In this example, n and a are being used as *flag variables*, for which some languages notably PASCAL, keeps a special type Boolean. In C, these variables would be of type integer or possibly char.

Oddly enough, though an integer variable needs two bytes for storage and only one bit is needed for this type of flag, it is often faster to specify int rather than char. A lot depends on your particular compiler here, but it's something to look out for. Note how an if test is placed in brackets and does not require the use of a THEN as in BASIC. The test if(n) by itself would mean 'if n not zero' and will give, like any other test, the result true (1) or false (0). Tests of this type are very common in C programs.

C expects you to enclose in brackets any test whose result will be true or false, so that tests such as the if test can be used. This rule is strictly applied, and can cause a lot of syntax errors to appear in your compilations at first until you get used to the idea. The || operator is used in a similar way, in a statement such as:

    if (name!= ' '||x)listit;

which means that if the character variable name is not a blank (represented by a space between two single quotes), or if integer x is not zero, then the function listit can run. Note that a character and an integer are both being tested.

For reasons that will be clearer later, you try to avoid making tests on strings, because there is *absolutely nothing* in C that corresponds to the BASIC test: IF A$ = B$ THEN . . . using an equality sign. To test two strings for equality in C requires the use of a library function that compares each character of one string with the corresponding character of the other, and gives the usual true or false results. The use of a $=$ test along with string names is virtually always an error, as we'll see when we come to strings in Chapter 9.

Operator precedence

The listing of operators in Figs 5.1 and 5.4 is in order of precedence in each list. As far as precedence of the list is concerned, the unary operators take precedence over the binary operators. This is the normal arrangement that you would expect from working with BASIC, and another point that you would expect is that in an expression where operators are of equal precedence the expression order is left to right. If you have any doubts, or if you want to impose your own precedence, you should use brackets so that whatever is enclosed in the brackets has precedence over whatever is outside the brackets. Unlike interpreted BASIC in which each set of brackets will slow down the action of the interpreter, the C compiler will convert your bracketed expession into fast running code no matter how you dress up your variables in brackets in the source code. One thing you must not take for granted, however is the order in which a compiler will deal with different parts of an expression.

If, for example, you have an expression in which a character is taken from a file in two different parts of a single expression, you can't depend on these actions taking place in the order that you would expect, left to right. There is nothing in the specification of C that guarantees this order of evaluation of an expression, and what actually happens will depend very much on the compiler that you are using, and may not even be consistent. If in doubt on such (rare) cases, it's better to split such an expression into two separate lines.

The ternary operator

C has one ternary operator, meaning an operator that deals with three items. The ternary operator is a conditional which allows two possible results of a test to be carried out in one statement. The syntax is:

    expression 1 ? result 1 : result 0

and the effect is to test expression 1. If this gives true (non-zero), then the result of the operator is result 1. If the tested expression gives false (0), then the result is result 0. These 'results' can be expressions also, and the effect is to carry out the equivalent of two tests in one compact statement.

Other operators

The sizeof operator is one that is quite definitely a stranger to BASIC. Its use is to determine how many bytes of storage a variable uses, and as such it comes in useful later on when we need to make room for variables. Normally, this is something that would not concern you, but in some C applications the variable storage size has to be specified. By using sizeof you can place the number into the expression automatically, saving you from having to calculate it for yourself. The sizeof operator comes into its own when we are working with structure variables, and we shall meet it in Chapter 10. Another operator, cast, will be dealt with in more detail in Chapter 6.

The binary code operations

The binary code operations have been kept until last in this chapter because they are not needed so much as the number and the character operations. I'll assume here that you have a working knowledge of binary code, because if you haven't, then this is no place to start learning, and it would be better to skip the rest of this chapter. This will not make you any less proficient with C, though it may debar you from working with some types of utility programs. You can learn about binary codes from any of the books on machine-code programming that apply to your computer.

The bitwise NOT operator uses the ˜symbol, and is unary. Its effect is to invert each bit of a byte, so that the result is the one's complement of the number. For example, suppose that you have a char number whose value is 65 denary. In binary code, this is 01000001. Performing the NOT action on this gives 10111110, which is in denary 190 or − 66, depending on how your compiler treats numbers like this. The effect of ˜65 with Zorland C is to give − 66.

The bitwise shifts $\gg$ and $\ll$ will shift the digits in a binary number by the number of places that is specified in the right-hand part of the expressions. For example, val $\ll$ 3 means that the binary number quantity represented by val will be shifted three places left. If val is the number 01100101, equivalent to 101 denary, then the result of the shifting action will be 00101000, 40 denary. If no digits are lost from the left-hand side of a binary number, then the result of a single place shift is multiplication by 2, but this can go very far adrift if one or more 1s are lost from the left-hand side of the number. The result that you will get, then depends on the number of places shifted and whether the number is of char size, or integer or long integer.

The example above uses a single byte by way of demonstration, but if an integer number is used, then the result is denary 808 as Fig. 5.5 shows.

Number before shifting:	0000	0000	0110	0101
Number after shifting:	0000	0011	0010	0111
(which is denary 808)				

Figure 5.5 The effect of three left shifts on the denary number 101, as illustrated on the binary equivalent.

Unless you choose to have both input and output in char form, the default is always integer. The $\gg$ sign operates to provide a bitwise shift right, equivalent to division by two with the remainder discarded.

The bitwise logic operators &, | and ^ have their usual truth-table actions, and Fig. 5.6 reminds you of these tables which apply to each bit in a byte. These logic actions are binary operators which compare a bit in each byte (or pair of bytes) with the corresponding bit in another byte or pair of bytes. Note that these actions are carried out on character and

AND (&) action on bits A, B, giving result Q:

A	B	Q
0	0	0
0	1	0
1	0	0
1	1	1

OR (|) action on bits A, B, giving result Q:

A	B	Q
0	0	0
0	1	1
1	0	1
1	1	1

XOR (^) action bits A, B, giving Q:

A	B	Q
0	0	0
0	1	1
1	0	1
1	1	0

Note: bits in a byte are numbered from 0, starting at the right-hand side.

Figure 5.6 The actions of AND, OR and XOR on single bits.

integer variables, not on floats. Their uses are mainly in masking and in encryption actions. For example, bit 7 of a number can be stripped by ANDing with the number hexadecimal 7F (written as 0X7F with a leading zero, or as \xff on some compilers), so that if we take the number denary 223 and AND with 127 (denary 7F) then the result is 95. In C terms:

    printf("%d",223&127);

will give this answer of 95. This is the way that a file of text from WordStar (to take one very well known example) can be converted into an ordinary ASCII file. If we wanted to set the most significant bit, still using a single byte number as an example, then the procedure is to OR with 0X80, in denary terms 128. For example, the result of:

    printf("%d",95|128);

will be 223 again, since this action resets bit 7 of the number. Figure 5.7 makes this example clearer by showing it in binary terms.

Denary 95 is binary	0101	1111 (8-bit char size)
Denary 128 is binary	1000	0000
Result of OR is	1101	1111
which is 223 in denary		

Figure 5.7 Explaining why the XOR of 95 with 128 is 223 – each bit in one number is XOR'd with the corresponding bit in the other number.

These two actions are most likely to be useful when applied to char variables, acting on the ASCII codes. You can mask out bit 7 to convert from WordStar form to pure ASCII, or to ensure that no graphics characters are sent to a printer or through a serial link. You can equally easily change between upper-case and lower-case, using bit 5, as Fig. 5.8 shows.

Letter G is coded as ASCII 71, binary	0100	0111
Letter g is coded as ASCII 103, binary	0110	0000

Bit 5 is 0 for upper-case, 1 for lower-case

To change lower-case to upper-case, use XOR 32 (^32).
To change upper-case to lower-case, use OR 32 (|32).

These actions are obtained by the toupper and tolower functions in most libraries.

Figure 5.8 How ASCII code uses bit 5 to distinguish between upper-case and lower-case letters.

Coding action:			
Byte to be coded	0100	0001	(8-bit char shown)
Code key	0100	1101	
Result of ~	0000	1100	

Decoding action:			
Code number	0000	1100	
Code key	0100	1101	
Result of ~	0100	0001	original code

Figure 5.9 Coding and decoding a byte with the aid of the XOR action.

The use of the XOR action for coding characters is well known, but that doesn't ensure that you have necessarily heard about it. The principle is that if a byte is XOR'd with another (key) byte, then the result is a code for the first byte. If this code is then XOR'd with the key byte again, the original byte is recovered. The encoding action is not confined to one step. If you use a double key, XORing the original byte with one key byte and then with another, the original can be recovered by two XOR actions, using the key bytes in either order. Figure 5.9 shows this in more detail, using a single byte example. Codings of this type, using a word code can be useful for many applications. The word can be used as a circulating letter sequence as Fig. 5.10 shows, or by using each letter of a word in sequence to XOR each character of the message, Fig. 5.11. On a simpler level, you can use a single character key for the first XOR and the same byte shifted one place left for the second XOR, reversing this process on the decoding action for each character.

Message is: T H E   M E S S A G E
Key is: K E Y K E Y K E Y K E

Results will be number codes, as for example 'T~'K' = 31, for each character. Repeating the action gives the original codes.

Figure 5.10 Using a key word, here shown as KEY, to code each letter and space of a message.

The results of all this might not keep the CIA out for long, but they are not so easy to break that any amateur is likely to get to your message in a

Message is: M E S S A G E
Key: K K K K K K K
         E E E E E E E
         Y Y Y Y Y Y Y

so that, taking the first letter, the ASCII code for 'M' is XORed with 'K', then the result with 'E', and this result with 'Y' to give the number 26. If this final code is then XORed with the codes for KEY in any order, the original byte will be recovered.

Figure 5.11 Using the characters of a key word in sequence on each character of a message.

moment or so unless your key is a very predictable one. The only point to watch is that the results of an encryption do not go outside the ASCII range. For example, if you use:

    printf("%c",'A'^'F');

to print as a character the XOR of ASCII A and ASCII F, then the result is a beep, the bell character 07. This is not a printing character, so it makes transmission of the message rather difficult. You may find, then that more than one XOR is needed on each character just to ensure that the code ends up in the correct range, and this makes the encryption rather complicated, because you have to make certain that each step is reversible, particularly if you have added AND stages to remove some 1 bits.

6
Types and Functions

Number type conversions

We have already looked at one form of the automatic conversion of types, the conversion of numbers in an expression so that each number type is converted to the most complex type used. The principle behind this is that no action on numbers should be made impossible just because the numbers happen to be of different types, and rather similar principles operate in BASIC, though you are seldom aware of what is going on. It is not difficult to see the sense of an arrangement when you want to add a float like 24.76 to an integer like 21 and get as a result the float 45.76. In this case of type conversion, it would be ridiculous if we needed any special instructions to carry out the conversion of the int to a float before performing the addition, yet this is just what is implied in a language that is described as being *strongly typed*, that no mixing of different types can be done.

In C, any conversion that makes reasonable sense is performed automatically, and only silly conversions are refused. To give the standard example, you won't be allowed to use floating-point numbers as the subscripts of an array. Where the BASIC programmer finds difficulty, however, is in the equally automatic promotion of a char variable of one byte to an integer of two bytes when these two types can be mixed. A conversion of this type can, for example, take the place of the BASIC STR$ statement. Consider, for example, the action:

J% = STR$(D$)

in BASIC, where D$ is assigned with "5". The C equivalent of this is simply:

j = d – '0';

with j being assigned with the ASCII code that is contained in d, minus the ASCII code for zero. This assumes that j is an integer variable and d is a char variable, and these variable types would, of course, have been declared earlier in the program.

Complex assignment

Assignment in BASIC amounts to something of the form (LET)X = expression, whether you are dealing with numbers or with strings. Strings are treated very differently in C, as you will find later, but number variable assignment can be as straightforward as that of BASIC. In addition, though, you can assign a variable in a way that in BASIC would need an expression. For example, in BASIC you might use:

X=X+2

but in C this could be written (and usually is written) as:

X+=2;

which looks like a straight assignment. Similarly the C statement:

X*=5

means the equivalent of BASIC X = X*5, that the new value of X is five times the old value. All of the arithmetic operators can be used along with the equality sign in this way which makes for compact listing at (initially at least) the expense of readability. You will from this point on see examples of this type of reassignment used in listings.

Another action that we now have to examine is *type coercion*. As the name implies, this means a type change that is not automatic and which we force by using a statement. The other name for this action is a *cast*. When you perform a cast, it is because you need to work on a number which will not be automatically converted into the type you want to use. A typical cast statement would take the form:

x = (unsigned)p;

in which the variable p would (typically) be of the pointer type. A pointer uses two bytes, just like an integer, but its type is not integer, nor is it automatically converted to integer. The cast statement here, using the brackets to contain the type to which the conversion is to be made, converts the pointer variable into an unsigned (integer) type and then assigns this to x, so that x must have been declared as an unsigned integer. This type of cast will always be necessary if you want to mix pointer numbers with others, since there is no automatic conversion of pointers (just as well, as you'll see) into other types of number variables. If you omit a cast action, the error message that you get may not be one that reminds you immediately of the error. A few compilers give a 'Bad type combination' error message, which is pretty unequivocal, but you are more likely to get 'illegal pointer arithmetic' or 'pointer mismatch' as reminders of what you are trying to do rather then just as a reminder of omitting a cast. If, however, you perform a cast incorrectly, you will get the 'illegal cast' message.

Functions

We have seen already that a program consists of any #define and
#include lines, then a main () which is followed by the opening curly
bracket, some statements, and then a closing curly bracket. In the main
program, between the curly brackets, you will place in sequence all the
actions that the program will carry out. Now in short programs, these
actions will be simple ones and they can all be written between the curly
brackets of the main program. As your programs become longer, however, you will need to break them into sections, if only for the sake of
effective planning. Just as you would (I hope) break a BASIC program
into a core and a set of subroutines, you break a C program into its main
and a set of other functions. The similarity between the languages ends
there, though. A function in C is called by using a name, its identifier,
which must be unique to that function.

In addition, values can be passed to a functions in ways that are not
used by subroutines in most PC types of BASIC. The use of a function is
therefore something that needs rather more thought than the use of a
subroutine. Unlike BASIC, C permits *only* functions, and there is nothing remotely like a subroutine. If you have programmed with defined
functions in a BASIC that used them (as all PC BASIC varieties do) then
you will feel more at home with the way that C uses functions.

```
#include <stdio.h>
/* needed for putchar */
main()
{
printf("\n The name is ");
attention('I'); /* function called */
}
attention(n) */ function defined here */
char n;
{
putchar(7); /* sound beep */
printf("%c",n);
printf(" Sinclair.");
putchar(7);
}
```

Figure 6.1 Calling a function, and illustrating how this function has to be
written.

Take a look, for example, at the program in Fig. 6.1. I have not typed this with indentation because it is such a simple program that you can see the separate parts of it without the need for indenting sections. This example starts in the usual way, and prints a phrase, 'The name is '. It then calls a function attention. Now this is not a function that is contained in the library, it is one that we have to write for ourselves and make available in the program. The name of the function is attention and it will make use of anything that is enclosed in the brackets. What is in the brackets in this instance is a character 'I'. Note that this is 'I' with a single quote mark, not "I" in double quotes as you would use in BASIC. The difference is very important. The 'I' is a character with an ASCII code of 73, whereas "I" would represent a string, and a string can never be of just one character unless it is an empty string as we'll see later. The 'I' is the argument of the function attention, the value that has to be passed for the function to use.

Now, of course, we can't compile this program and run it until there is a function attention written and available to the compiler. The main() program is ended with its second curly bracket, and following it we type the name of the function, which is attention(n). We can make the letter inside the brackets anything we like, it can be a complete name or just a single letter as shown here. We then have to declare this letter n, unless it has been declared elsewhere globally, showing that this variable will hold a character. The curly bracket then opens, there is a statement putchar(7) and then the character is printed. Now this character is represented in the first printf line as n. This is a variable name which in this example exists only inside this function, and because n was used in the 'header' as the argument of function attention (), it takes the value that was used as an argument when the function was called, which is 'I'. The printf modifier is %c, meaning that the variable which follows will be printed as a single ASCII character. The next line is a conventional printf – notice that we don't need a modifier because we don't want a new line and we are not printing a variable, just a phrase within quotes. The last part of this function is then another putchar(7). These putchar functions are standard parts of a C library, and can be consulted in your compiler manual. You will almost certainly have to use the #include < stdio.h > line in your program to make use of putchar(7), which is the equivalent of BASIC PRINTCHAR$(7), the beep sound.

Now when you compile and run, you see the complete phrase appear on the screen. It would, of course, have been just as easy to use the whole phrase in a printf line in the main program, but it's always easier to see how something works from a simple example than from a complicated one. The important point is that any function that you want to use can be called up by using its name, and the brackets are used to pass any arguments to the function. These arguments can be integers, floats, characters or strings used direct as variable names or, as we shall later, as pointers. When the function itself is written, you write it like another main() type of program with the exception of the declaration that is needed before the opening curly bracket.

In this example, this has meant calling up other functions putchar and printf which exist in the library on your disk (in Zorland C, this library is placed on the disk that contains your program file). This is typical of the way that we write program in C – a small main() program calls up functions which in turn call up other functions and so on. You can use the TYPE action of MS-DOS to look at the demonstration programs that come with your compiler, and you'll see just how short the main() program is in most cases. Note that many programmers place the main() program at the end of the text. This is a matter of preference in C; though many languages like PASCAL insist that the main program code is placed at the end of the text, C allows you to put main() at the beginning if you like. I prefer main to be at the beginning because it makes the purpose of the program clear on the first page. A few function types may have to be placed before main() for some purposes, but that's not something you need to worry about in the early stages of learning C.

The variable n in this example exists only within the attention function. If you try to print its value near the end of the program, following the attention('I'); line, you will find that you get an error message about 'undefined identifier' when you try to compile. This means that n was not declared as a variable at the start of the main() function. The fact that it has been declared as a char type in the function attention refers to this function only, and you can print a value of n at any time in the course of function attention. The significance of this is that you provided a value of 'I' as the argument for attention.

This *value* is then temporarily transferred to variable n for the duration of the function only. The transfer is completely automatic, and is rather different from the methods that you may have encountered in BASIC. The description of n and anything of this type is a *local variable*, and very few varieties of BASIC permit anything of this sort to be used. All of the variables that are declared inside a C function are automatically made local to that function. We'll look later at the principles of passing back values from a function and of using global variables whose values are retained in all parts of a program.

Header and body

One simple example can't serve to show everything about a C functions, and Fig. 6.2 illustrates the more general layout of a function. The first two lines here, preceding the curly bracket, constitute the *header* of the function which defines what the function is intended to do. The portion

```
function type name (argument list)
declare variables passed to the function
{
declare other variables
main body of statements
return(value) [optional]
}
```

Figure 6.2 The general layout of a function. The portion up to the opening curly bracket is known as the header of the function.

that is placed between the curly brackets is the body of the function, the statements that carry out the actions of the function. The only point that we need to note about the *body* of the function at present is that it consists of any declaration that has not been made in the header, and of statements which may or may not include a return statement. The return statement is closely bound up with what appears in the header, and we'll ignore it for now. It has no connection with the RETURN that you may have used at the end of a BASIC subroutine.

The header of a C function has to be designed in a fairly rigidly specified way. The first word in the header is the type of function, meaning the type of quantity that the function will return to main(). For many functions, either nothing is returned, or the return is of an integer, and the default is integer. Modern practice is always to show what the function returns, using void if it returns nothing, and int if it returns an integer. In this way, you are always reminded of what a function will return.

The point about automatically returning an integer, incidentally, means that if a char is returned, it will have been converted into integer form. If the function returns anything else, such as an unsigned, a float or double, then this must be stated in the header, and if you don't want a char to be changed to int, then you have to put in char as the type for the function. Failure to do so will cause an integer to be returned (if anything is returned), and this might possibly cause you problems.

The next part of the header consists of the function name and its argument list. The name can be any name that you choose, subject to the normal rules about alphabetical and numerical characters, use of the underline, and possible conflicts with existing library function names. Obviously you have to avoid the use of names of other existing functions and the reserved names of C, and as we noted earlier, it's highly advisable to keep clear of any names that start with the underline character.

Following the name of the function, and enclosed in round brackets, come the arguments, the list of variable names for quantities that will be passed to the function. These, remember, need not be identical to the names that you will use when you call the function from main(). You can have a function header that starts with:

> int getit(a,b,c)

and call it with getit(brand,product,price) or ("Wizard","broom-sticks", 5.60), provided that the variables or supplied quantities are of the correct type and in the correct order. If your function header contains three arguments that are two ints and a char, then you cannot expect it to work correctly if you call it with two chars and an int in that order. Each and every variable that has to be passed to the function must be included in this argument list.

Having dealt with the argument list, the argument declarations then follow on logically. In this part of the header, each argument must have its type declared. There are no defaults here; if you have put a variable name in the arguments list then its type must appear in the declaration unless a global variable was used.

Finally, we return to the body of the function. This can include any declarations, particularly of variables that will be used only in the function, but this can also include a variable whose value will be returned. If, for example, you have near the end of a function the line:

> return(x);

then this means that the value of variable x at this point will be returned as the function value.

If the returned value x is an integer, and the function was declared as being of int type, then this returned value can be printed or assigned. Suppose, for example, that the function name was calcit, declared in its header as type int and with a return(x) line. If you called this function by using printf(calcit), then the effect of this call would be to print the value of x at the time when the return(x) statement was executed. You cannot, however, use a sequence such as:

> calcit;
> printf("%d",x);

because the value of x is local to the function, it does not exist or is used in a different meaning in the main program or in another function. If you want to print the value of x, you can use:

> printf("%d",calcit());

or if you want to assign the value of x to something else you can use a statement such as:

> y=calcit();

assuming that the variable y had been declared as an int variable. Obviously if calcit had been declared as being of type float, then the variable y would need to be also of this type, and if you used the printf form, then the specifier %d will be replaced by %f. You can, incidentally, use return with no variable and no brackets. Its effect will then be to force the function to end at this point rather than at the closing curly bracket. This is used mainly in testing a function to see what happens if a later portion is omitted.

Local and global variables

Unless you have had the fortune to use a BASIC that allows local variables (or have programmed PASCAL), this is probably one item in C that will cause you a lot of head scratching. As usual in C, the rules are

```
int x=5; /* global value */
main()
{
printf("\n%d",x);
test();
try();
prove();
printf("\n%d",x);
}
test()
{
printf("\n%d",x);
}
try()
{
int x;
printf("\n%d",x);
}
prove()
{
int x;
x=6;
printf("\n%d",x);
}
```

Figure 6.3 A program that illustrates the rules regarding a global variable.

quite straightforward, but when you are converting from a language that does not have such rules, you need to think about what you are doing. Running through an example is, as usual, the best way to understand what is going on.

In addition, there is the matter of what happens when C tries to be obliging about something that doesn't exist. Figure 6.3 shows a listing which consists of a main() with three other functions. None of the functions has a value passed to it, because the one variable that is used is declared and assigned outside main, before the word main() appears, making it global to the main function and therefore to everything else that is called from main. The important thing is to recognise just how global a global variable is. Any variable that is declared outside a function will be global to all of the functions that are called by that function. Such a variable would not, however, be global to any functions that were used before it was defined, or which exist outside the function in which the definition was included. The most global function that you can get, then, is one that is defined before the start of main.

The listing of Fig. 6.3 starts with a declaration, int x=5; which makes x an integer, with a value of 5, that will be global for the whole program. The main() is then started. The value of x is then printed to prove that it exists. The function test is then called. This function does no more than print the value of x. The variable name of x has not been declared in the function, nor has any value been assigned. Because of that, the value is still the global one, and that's what the function prints.

The next function is try. This time, variable x is declared as an integer, but no assignment is made. The value is then printed, and when this runs, what is printed depends entirely on what happens to be in the memory that your compiler has laid aside for this variable – the test with Zorland C on the Amstrad PC produced 266. The global value of 5 is quite definitely not printed, because of the declaration that creates a new local variable x. By declaring int x in the function header we have over-ruled the global variable x in the main program, but since this local x has not been assigned with a value, only with a space in the memory, then what is printed is whatever happens to be in that piece of memory. This is highly likely (almost inevitably) to be garbage, and the point is important. When an auto variable is used without initialisation, the value will always be garbage. If you use a static variable without initialisation, then the compiler will usually initialise to zero. Unlike BASIC, however, you can find that uninitialised variables can print some remarkable garbage.

In the function prove, the value of x is declared and assigned with 6. The printout, as you would expect, is 6 this time. Once more, the global value of x has been temporarily overruled – the word that is used is 'hidden' – and the new value for x has been correctly assigned. When

(a)	(b)	(c)
5	5	5
5	10	10
265	268	265
6	6	6
5	10	6

Figure 6.4 Printouts from the listing of Fig. 6.3. (a) The listing as printed, (b) after adding x = 2 ∗ x (or x ∗ = 2) just before the printf line in function test. (c) The result of deleting the int x step in function prove.

function prove returns to main, the value of x is printed again and is once again the global value of 5. The assignment of 6 within the function prove has had no effect on this. Figure 6.4(a) shows the set of numbers that will be printed as the program runs.

A global variable, then, is global only if no other function declares a variable of the same name. A function can alter the value of a global variable, and the altered value will be used from then on, just as you would expect from BASIC experience. If we add another line to the function test, just before the printf line, using:

x ∗ = 2;

then the printout will be as in Fig. 6.4(b). The new value of 10 in the function is printed, and this value of 10 is now the value of the global variable and persists outside the function after the change has been made. Finally, try deleting the int x step in function prove. This assigns a new value to global variable x rather than to local variable x as it did before, and the result of this will be that the new value of 6 will be retained at the end of the program as Fig. 6.4(c) shows.

To summarise then, we can pass values to and from functions in two distinct ways so far. The conventional way is to pass values in a header, and pass one value back by way of the return statement. We can pass more than one value back by way of pointers, as we shall see later. The less conventional method, which is the more familiar method for the BASIC programmer, is to use global variables that can be passed to and from functions, altered or not. This may look more useful, but it's a method that C programmers try to avoid as far as possible. The reason is that it's too easy to lose track of global variables. One or two such variables might perhaps be acceptable, but in a program that might typically contain several hundred functions, some of which will be taken from the library, the use of global variables is a nuisance at best, and a prolific source of bugs at worst.

You should therefore try to wean yourself away from the temptations of global variables so that you can write your C functions in units that you can collect into a library and use in all of your programs without modification. All of this, then, leads us to consider what is contained in a C library.

The library

The library is one of the glories of C, because it's the way in which the language can be continually extended and made more useful. The library is a set of functions, initially written in source code, then compiled into object code and stored in sequence. Its value is that any function in the library can be named in your program, and taken from the library disc to be included by the linker into your program. In a few versions of C, this has to be done by adding the library functions in source code and then compiling, but all of the C compilers for the PC use the more conventional object code library functions, which take up much less disk space.

In addition to the functions that are held as object code in the library, there are files which are held separately in source code and which are used as headers for the library files. These are the files with the .h extension, such as stdio.h. Files like this are needed in order to make use of library files and they must be placed right at the start of a program, before anything else, even before the #define lines. The stdio header, for example, is installed by typing:

> #include stdio.h

The use of #include with a filename like this causes the compiler to look on the disc for the routines. The stdio.h file, being in source code, can be printed out (by using TYPE under DOS, for example, or from an editor or word processor), and you will see that it includes lines such as:

> #define EOF – 1
> #define NULL 0

and other lines of this type that are used by the library routines. It will also contain the function headers which show the function type and the form of variables that will have to be passed to the function. Take a look at your own stdio.h file, and don't be surprised at the size of this file.

As far as the main library is concerned, it's likely that your compiler will follow the same path as others and provide a library manager program. This program allows for a listing of the library contents, as well as for alterations in the form of additions, deletions and substitutions. What is provided depends very much on the compiler that you use, and Fig. 6.5 shows the use of the ZORLIB program for maintaining the Zorland NL.LIB object code library.

Zorlib is a library maintenance program that allows you to survey the contents of the library (names of routines), add, remove, or copy object code files. You can also create a new library.

The ZORLIB command can include all your requirements into one command line, but a simpler method of use is to type ZORLIB, and answer the three prompts that then appear. The first prompt is for the name (including disk drive and path if applicable) for the library. The second is for any files that you want to work on, and the third is for the output listing (screen, file, printer). A complicated set of commands that you use frequently can be combined into a response file (like a batch file).

Figure 6.5 Outline of the Zorlib library manager program.

The next step is to decide what to use from the library. You will find as you go along that most of the routine that you need to use are library routines, particularly as regards string handling. Some routines can be dealt with in the header, without the need to make a very extensive call to the library, certainly not where you would expect it. For example, if you look in the Zorland stdio.h you will find the line:

#define getche() bdos(1)   /* get char from kbd, echo it */

which shows the definition of the function getche() as a #define line in the stdio.h file. What this amounts to is that wherever you use the getche() in a program, the pre-processor will substitute the bdos(1) function from the library, which is a call direct to the MS-DOS operating system. This means that the library can be smaller than you might expect, because many of the functions of C can be interpreted as calls to MS-DOS or as modified versions of other C functions.

For most purposes, however, you can get the library information that you need from your compiler manual. The entry in the Zorland manual for the function atoi, for example, starts:

    int atoi(string)
    char *string

meaning that atoi is a function that returns an integer and which takes as its argument a string. It is one equivalent for the BASIC VAL(string) command, the other being atof (for floats), and for the moment we'll ignore the char *string whose meaning will become clearer later when we have looked at pointers. The atoi functions requires no #include <stdio.h>, so the program example of Fig. 6.6 starts with a #define line which defines a string constant as "123fg". The function is the one

```
#define sample "123fg"
main()
{
int val;
val=atoi(sample);
printf("\n Value is %d",val);
}
```

Figure 6.6   Finding the integer numeric value of a string, using the atoi function.

that provides the conversion of a string of digits into an integer number, and ignores any non-digit characters. Only the number characters at the start of the string are converted, just like the VAL action in BASIC. In this example, the string is a string constant, and the atoi action converts it into an integer 123, which is printed in the usual way. There are many more functions which will act on strings, but before we can make really effective use of them, we need to be able to work with pointers, the crowning glory of C. That's for later!

Planning

One of the most important points about functions is how they affect the

Figure 6.7   A popular planning method outlined. The main objectives are listed at the left-hand side, and each main step is then broken into finer detail, using curly brackets to connect the steps. The finest detail is on the right-hand side of the diagram.

planning of programs. How, for example, do we plan the simple illustration of Fig. 6.1? Figure 6.7 illustrates a version of one method which is favoured by many programmers. The left-hand side shows the steps of the main program, with the main action shown as one step. The curly brackets are then used to show where more details are needed. This has been used in the example to show variable names, and also to show what has to be done in each function. The important point is that a function is designed in very much the same way as the main program is designed. You can design a function without constantly having to refer to the main program, because the variables that are used within a function need not bear the same names as these used in the main program, the only essential feature is that they should be of the same type. In general, if you define variables for the main program at the start of the program, these variables can also be used in the function. If you define variables inside a function, these variables are 'local', they are used only in the function, and simply don't exist when the function is not running.

More planning

Let's look now at a short program, starting with the design steps. This is to be a program which will convert a list of metric dimensions in millimetres into the inch equivalents. The planning, such as it is, is shown in Fig. 6.8. On the left-hand side, the main steps of the program are listed as Start, declare, loop, action and End. The curly brackets now open into more detail. The variables will be called mm and inch and while the mm numbers can be integers, the inch numbers will have to be floats. The range and steps will be dealt with by using a loop, which is something new for us. The only detail which is included in this list is the range of dimensions, 0 to 100 in steps of 5 mm. The conversion could be done by a

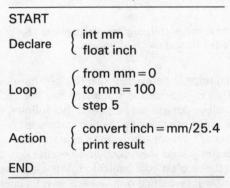

START

Declare { int mm
          float inch

Loop { from mm = 0
       to mm = 100
       step 5

Action { convert inch = mm/25.4
         print result

END

Figure 6.8 The diagram used to plan a simple mm to inch converter.

function, but it's so simple that it's hardly worth while, and we simply use the conversion formula. The #define line is used to put in the constant 25.4 which is the number of millimetres per inch, and the #include math.h is needed in Zorland C for the maths header that will be used with the floating point numbers.

Now this program illustrates that a FOR loop in C takes a very different form, particularly as regards the STEP portion. Figure 6.9 shows the program which has been drawn up from the plan. As always, looking at a finished program gives you no idea of what the steps were in writing it, so we'll look at the program in the order in which it was written. The main program starts in the usual way with main(), and then declares the integer mm and the float inch. Remember that in the main() program, this type of declaration must be carried out following the first curly bracket, unlike declaration of argument variables in other functions. The next step is the loop which carries out the actions of converting and printing the values.

```
#include <math.h>
/* needed for working with floats */
#define mmin 25.4
main()
{
int mm;
float inch;
for (mm=0;mm<=100;mm+=5)
  {
   inch=mm/mmin;
   printf("\n%d mm is %f inches",mm,inch);
  }
}
```

Figure 6.9   The listing of the program which prints a list of mm and corresponding inch sizes for the range of values.

Now the first thing to note here is that the loop line does not end with a semicolon. This is because the statement has not ended, we have to specify what will be done in the loop, and that follows, enclosed in curly brackets. The effect of enclosing the two statements in curly brackets is to make this set of lines constitute one single statement. A set like this is often called a *compound statement*, and because it ends with a closing curly bracket, it doesn't need a semicolon. What is inside this set of curly brackets, then, will be carried out on each pass through the loop.

The next thing to look at very carefully is how the loop statement is constructed. In many ways, this corresponds well to the BASIC statement:

FOR C=0 TO 100 STEP 5

but C writes this as a set of conditions. The first test is mm = 0, the starting condition for the loop. The next is mm < = 100, meaning mm less than 100 or equal to 100. This is the ending condition. The third is mm + = 5 (or mm = mm + 5), and this is the stepping condition. If you think that it is all very clear and straightforward, then try omitting the step condition. You'll find that the loop is then endless, and you need to use Ctrl Break to get out of it. Unless you put in a step condition, there won't be one, and the loop will be endless, unless variable mm gets incremented somewhere within the curly brackets following the loop statement. Unlike BASIC, C provides you with no default step size of unity.

The other difference from BASIC is the condition mm < = 100. If you try making this mm = 100, you'll find the loop goes only as far as 95, because after 95, the value of mm is not less than 100. Now try making the middle condition mm = 100, and see what this does. The effect, another endless loop, is most unexpected if you are still thinking in BASIC terms. The reason is that each part of the loop statement is a condition. The mm = 0 part is a starting condition and the mm < = 100 is an ending condition, but the loop does not end until this condition is FALSE. If you put in a condition which makes the loop impossible, the result is an endless loop. With mm=0 and (mm=100) both false, the loop should not run, and the response is to increment mm to 100, then run continuously! The conditions x < number, x > number, x < = number, or x > = number are the ones that you should always use for a loop of this type, using x to represent a number variable. Since C offers you the choice of two other loops, you can't really complain that you are restricted for choice.

The conversion to inches uses the constant mmin, and assigns the result to variable name inch and is the first action in the loop. The next action is to print both amounts. With the range of quantities that we have chosen, there will nearly always be a fractional result, so that the number of decimal places may have to be specified. This has not been done in this example, so that the way that the numbers are presented could be improved. Another improvement is to use left-justification, and this can be done by using the line:

printf("\n% – 3d mm is %f inches",mm,inch);

which lines up the printing of the words. This isn't perfect, though, because we don't normally left-justify numbers. A better display is obtained by using:

print("\n   %3d mm is %f3.2 inches",mm,inch);

which looks a lot better. Three spaces have been typed between 'n' and
'%', and the first number has been right-justified to three figures. This
puts the number always hard against the right side of the spaces that you
have left for it, and makes the display look better. The floating-point
number is printed with a maximum of three digits preceding the point
(no more than one is needed in this range) and two digits following the
point, as commanded by using %f3.2.

More functions

It's time to take another look at a function action, one which is simple
but rewarding to consider. This time, as the listing of Fig. 6.10 shows, the
function is called (or *invoked*) as part of a printf statement. The other
important point which this program illustrates is one way in which a
value can be passed back from a function. The loop makes use of
numbers from 0 to 10, and the incrementing is taken care of by using
x+ + as the third term in the for statement.

```
main ()
{
int x;
for (x=0;x<=10;x++)
printf("\n%d cubed is %d",x,cube(x));
}
cube(a)
int a;
{
return(a*a*a);
}
```

Figure 6.10   A function which returns a value by way of the return
statement.

Since there is only one statement in the loop, it can follow the for part,
and be terminated with a semicolon which now marks the end of the
loop. If you put the semicolon after the for statement you'll get a loop,
but with nothing in it! The printf statement prints the value of x, and
also the value of cube(x). Now cube(x) is a function which in this case
returns an integer, so we have to define it somewhere, but the main point
is how it comes to have a number value. The answer is in the line
return(a*a*a);. This means that a value is to be given to the function,
and that value is a*a*a, the cube of a number which has been assigned
to variable a. Remember that a is local to the function, it has no value in
the main program. The value of x is passed to a when the function starts,
and the function therefore acquires the value of x*x*x at the return step
– there is no change to the value of x.

Once again, you are not forced to pass values to and from a function in this way. You could have declared and used x as a global variable in the way that has already been described. You might feel more familiar with such a method, but by using it you shut yourself off from the ability to make this cube routine one of your library routines that you can use again in any of your programs. That is the whole point of functions in C as compared to subroutines in BASIC.

A BASIC subroutine, because of its line numbers and its global variables, will almost always have to be changed if it is used in a program other than the one for which it was originally intended. A C function is, by contrast, like a diamond, for ever. Providing that the function uses local variables and passes values out by using return or by the use of pointers, then it is a universal function and you can place it into any program without having to edit the function to change variable names or anything of the sort. Benefits like this are not to be thrown away just because you were brought up on global variables!

The comma operator

Since this book is aimed at the beginner, this item is one that you can skip first time around. In brief, the comma operator allows extra items to be put into a for loop, in particular in the step portion so that more than one step action can be included. The normal separators for the sections of a for loop are the semicolons, so that a comma can be used to indicate different step parts. Suppose, for example, that the loop includes the stages:

```
for (j = 0;j < = 100;j + +)
{
    n - - ;
    (rest of loop)
}
```

This can be shortened by putting in the decrementing of n along with the incrementing of j, using the comma between the items, as:

```
for (j = 0;j < = 100;j + + ,n - - )
{ rest of loop
}
```

Where the comma is used in this way, the expressions that are separated by commas are evaluated in a left to right order. In this particular example, there is nothing returned from the line that uses the comma, but if the comma has been used in a line that returns a value, only the expression on the extreme right, the last expression, yields a return value. This use of the comma is not the same as the use of the commas as a separator between items in a list.

7
Pointers

A pointer is a type of number variable, and the reason for its name is that it 'points' to where something is stored. For example, suppose that you have the character 'C' stored in the memory of the PC. What this actually means is that one of the memory cells is storing the number which is the ASCII code for C, the number (denary) 67. Now memory for a computer is organised so that each unit (or byte) is numbered, and we might know that the number of the byte which held our 'C' was 9400. This number of 9400, then, is the number which is the pointer for the storage of the character 'C', so that it is a pointer to type char. We could, if we liked, store the number 9400 somewhere so as to make it possible for the computer to find where 'C' was stored, and this is precisely what the action of a pointer is.

It would be rather a waste to store a pointer for every character, but we don't need to. All we need to do is to store a pointer to the start of any variable. Once we know where the start is, we can locate it and read the required number of bytes of data. This is something that is used a lot in assembly language programming, but seldom, occurs in BASIC for small computers. The main varieties of BASIC for the PC, however, have a BASIC function called VARPTR which comes back with a number that tells you where about in the memory a variable is stored. In BASIC, however, there is little use for this action, and not many programmers make use of it, or are even aware of it. In C, however, pointers are a way of storing variables and getting access to them. This is not just a useful feature of C, it's something that is central to the way that the language is constructed. Without pointers, you simply don't get very far with C. This is in marked contrast to the use of pointers in PASCAL, in which pointers are a useful ornament which you are very seldom obliged to use.

Take a look at a simple example just to get the taste of all this. Figure 7.1 is a program which declares two variables of type char. One of these variables is ccr, which is a straightforward variable name. The other, however, is referred to as *p. Now the asterisk, in this context means 'contents of'. What it implies is that p is an address in the memory, and a character, the contents, can be held at that address. At this stage, neither the address nor the character is defined. The program then assigns the variable ccr with 'C', a single ASCII code, and then assigns the pointer by using p = &ccr. The & operator, used in this context, means 'address of'. The effect, then, is to store the character C at a valid address, and then assign that same address number to the pointer p. The program then prints out the character, in the form *p, and the pointer value itself, which when I ran it on my machine gave 9366. You can expect different numbers to appear when you use pointers, because the number that appears depends on where the machine stored the variable ccr, and that's something between it and its maker. By using %u with printf to specify an unsigned integer, incidentally, we ensure that the number which is printed is positive. No conversion of the pointer number into an unsigned is needed in order to print a pointer in this way.

```
main()
{
char *p,cr; /* p is a pointer */
cr='X';
p=&cr; /* p must be assigned */
printf("\n%c",*p);
printf("\n%u",p);
}
```

Figure 7.1 A character and its pointer. The last line allows you to find what memory location (relative to segment start) is being used for the pointer in your machine.

A pointer in C is a variable quantity which is the address of another variable. What makes the pointer valuable is that if the pointer is declared, the compiler does not need to have the other variable declared. For example, if the pointer to a real number is known, and is variable, then the name of the real number does not have to appear earlier in the program. A pointer reserves space for a declared type of variable, what you put into the space later is your own business, provided that it's the correct variable type. In addition, the pointer is a number (unsigned), but what it points to can be any type of variable, simple (such as another integer) or structured (like a record which consists of a number of different types). We can then juggle with the pointers rather than with the variables themselves. The only fly in this useful ointment is that C does nothing to allocate pointer values sensibly; you have to assign values to your pointers or suffer the consequences.

All of this sounds rather academic, so take a look at an example which reveals a little of what all this is about. In Fig. 7.2, two integers x and y

80 *Simple C*

```
main()
{
 int x,y;
 x=10;
 square(x,&y); /* pass int and address of int */
 printf("\n%d %d",x,y);
}
square(x,p)
int *p; /* p gets value of &y passed to it */
{
 *p=x*x;
}
```

Figure 7.2 Passing a pointer to an integer so that a function can use the integer and alter the variable value.

are declared in the main program. The variable x is assigned with a value, but y is not. The function square(x,&y) is then called. The quantities that have been passed here are the variable x and its value, and the address of y.

The important item here is that we don't deal with y, simply its address pointer. In the function, the header declares that the content of pointer p is an integer, which is all we need in order to declare p itself. The value of p will be assigned as the address of y, but all this is implied rather than declared. We can then make the statement which assigns the contents of pointer p to the cube of number x, and the function ends there. Now if we had assigned y = x*x, then y, if it had been declared in the header of the function, would have been assigned this value, but it could not have passed it back unless you used the return statement. Using a pointer does allow a quantity to be returned in the form of its pointer address. This is because the pointer address has not been changed, only what it pointed to (contained). The main program then prints a value of y, using the pointer address of y, which has now been changed by the function to give the square of x.

Now this is strong stuff – the quantity that has been stored in a variable y has been changed without the need to have a line y = x*x, or even a direct reference to y, all that has been done is to pass &y, the pointer to y, to the function. This is the way in which a function can return values to a main program, and it's a method that is very extensively used in the C library functions. In order to make any substantial use of the library functions, we have to master this idea of using pointers. At the moment, one problem that has been hanging over us is how to enter numbers, so this seems a good time to introduce one way, the scanf function.

Now as it happens, scanf is not the easiest of functions to use, and a lot of novice programmers avoid it like the plague. The principles are reasonably straightforward, though, and it's principles that we want to look at. Function scanf is set out very much like printf, with a control section, and a list of the variables that you want to input. So far, it sounds just like good old BASIC INPUT A,B,C. The important difference is that scanf requires pointers to variables, not just variable names by themselves. The other thing, the one that causes a lot of frustration, is that scanf works to strict and rather old-fashioned rules, and can do the most amazing things if you don't understand the rules or forget how strictly they are applied.

```
main()
{
int j,k;
for(j=0;j<=5;j++)
  {
  printf("\n Small number please- ");
  scanf("%d",&k);
  k=k*k*k;
  printf("\n cube is %d",k);
  /* can omit \n to avoid blank line */
  }
}
```

Figure 7.3 Using a pointer with scanf, which forces you to work either with pointers directly or to pass an address of a variable with the & operator.

Figure 7.3 illustrates a scanf action, and gives you a taste of its use of pointers. The Zorland scanf is free of the peculiarities that I have encountered on one other variety on a very different machine, and adheres to C specifications. The main program sets up a loop which will run from 0 to 5 - 6 passes through the loop. In each loop, we want to print a brief message, input a number, calculate its cube, and then print that value. The input of the number is the action that is assigned to scanf, and the syntax for this particular example is:

scanf("%d",&k);

which at first sight, looks rather baffling. Run it, and check that it does as it ought to, remembering that all the arithmetic is integer, so that squaring large numbers will give very peculiar results. On the whole, it does as you might expect, though you'll notice that there has been an extra blank line. This is because of the use of (RETURN) to terminate the scanf line. You can miss out the \n portion of the second printf statement if you want to close it all up.

There are lot of possibilities here, but the important point to look at is how scanf deals with the address pointer to variable k. The quantity that is called for in scanf is &k, the pointer to k. The action of scanf is to assign the number that you type into this pointer, so that the variable k can be used with this value. It's a very good illustration of a function being used to work with a pointer, and scanf is a function which required that all of its returned values should be pointers. We'll come back to scanf later, but for the moment try editing the scanf line so that the specifier part reads ''%d%*c''. The %*c part makes the scanf action skip a character, and its effect in this case is to allow you to enter a number, but to hang up when you press RETURN, and wait until you press RETURN again.

From a brief description of pointers and scanf, it's only too easy to run away with the idea that this is something that is not really terribly difficult or tricky. A lot of newcomers read the 'standard' textbooks, feel that they know it all, and then sit down to write a ten line program which to their disgust, never seems to run correctly. This isn't due to any inherent difficulty with the language, it is mainly because it is so different from other languages, particularly BASIC, and because C allows you so much more latitude to make mistakes. You can do things in C that in BASIC would cause in instant error report. C allows you to do what you want, silly or not, and delivers the results, and if these results include wiping out half of the memory, then that's when you find out if you have blundered or not. In addition, textbooks tend to concentrate on what you *can* do, and skip over what you can't do. We'll take a look now at some ways in which you can go wrong, both with pointers and with scanf because these two are so closely linked together.

To start with, look at the two listings in Fig. 7.4(a) and 7.4(b). These look as if they are intended to do the same thing, to allow you to input a character and then print it on the screen. The difference is in the way that the character is defined and the pointer used. In Fig. 7.4(a) the declaration is the conventional char p, meaning that p represents a character, and assigning a suitable place in the memory for this character. In the scanf line we use &p, the address of (pointer to) the character p, as scanf requires. There is no problem, because the declaration of p as type char has also assigned an address, &p. When we print the character, we print it as p.

The alternative is a classic illustration of an error which can cause immense damage, yet be unnoticed; it's called an unassigned pointer error. This time the declaration is char *p, meaning that pointer address p will contain a character. The trouble is that this address p has not been chosen in any sensible way, and a compiler constructed to strict C rules will allocate a number more or less at random. This causes no problem at this stage, or if you change the address assigned to p, but it can cause trouble if you store anything in this address. You may be lucky, and find

```
main()
{
char p;
printf("\nType a character\n");
scanf("%c",&p); /* uses address of p */
printf("\n It was %c",p);
}                                                    (a)

main()
{
char *p;
printf("\nType a character\n");
scanf("%c",p);
/* danger - p is not assigned */
printf("\n It was %c",*p);
}
/* now restart in case of memory
   corruption */                                     (b)

main()
{
char *p;
printf("\n Type a character\n");
scanf("5c",&p); /* confusing p and *p */
printf("\n It was %c",*p);
}                                                    (c)
```

Figure 7.4 Character input and printing routines. (a) A correct method which declares a character variable and assigns the pointer to the variable address. (b) The main source of trouble in C – using a pointer which has not been assigned to any address. (c) Confusing a pointer and a variable; another common source of trouble.

that the address p is of a blank piece of memory. You may be unlucky and find that it is an address used by part of MS-DOS or by the C compiler. Apart from this, scanf can use p directly, and the printf line needs *p, the character stored in address p. Note that there is no variable of type char, only a pointer, and this in itself should always start alarm bells ringing. To repeat the point, unless some assigning action is used that will make the point point to some established address, then the point will generally point to garbage or to some important address that ought not to be changed. You can either assign the pointer to the established address, pass an address to the pointer in a function, or use a function (calloc or malloc) to allocate memory for a pointer. Do none of these and you will bury bugs into your program that will make their presence felt sooner or later. No C compiler will draw your attention to this 'unassigned pointer' error, and as far as I know, only the Living C interpreter catches this mistake.

These examples are important because one of the things that haunts newcomers to C is confusion between a variable and its pointer, a confusion that is made worse by the way that C deals with arrays. The distinction is particularly important when you use scanf, because scanf forces you to use pointers. One very common mistake is to use & and * the wrong way round, another is to confuse the pointer with what it points to. Just to make things more difficult, these confusions don't necessarily cause error messages to appear. Even more confusing than that is the fact that some mistaken listings may work! If a scanf line is followed by a printf line, as in this example, you can often see when something has gone wrong. If, for example, you typed the other incorrect version of Fig. 7.4(c) then it compiles and runs, but what you type is not what is printed. The reason is not exactly straightforward, but it can be explained if you make some intermediate printings by putting in a line:

```
printf("\n%u %u %u\n",p,*p,&p);
```

When this line runs, you will see that *p is the ASCII code for the character that appears on the screen, and the quantities p and &p are different numbers.

At the start, p has been declared as a pointer to a character. In the scanf line, what is supplied is &p, the address of the pointer itself. The character is therefore p, whether you like it or not, because that is determined by the action of scanf. The trouble here is that p has been declared as a pointer, which is a two-byte number, so that when you print p as an unsigned denary number it has a second byte which makes it look quite different from the character. In addition, this two byte number will point to somewhere in memory, so that *p will give some character, but certainly not the one you typed. C allows you to place and use any garbage that you like into the memory of the computer. You get no warning, no error messages providing that the syntax of your program is acceptable. If the garbage that you place then proceeds to zonk out the compiler or the operating system, then that's just too bad.

This means that if you program in a slap-happy way, as you tend to do with tolerant ol' BASIC, you will run into deep trouble at some stage. The worst type of trouble is that a program seems to work perfectly well, but the whole system crashes after some time. It's rather like a game of roulette, but in this case you are waiting for the memory corruption to hit something important. That is why it is so important to write C programs from tried and trusty routines.

After all that, it's time we did some more with scanf. The example of
Fig. 7.4(a) will accept any characters, including the whitespace character
of space, tab and RETURN key. The scanf statement in this case reads
one character and one only. When we come to deal with arrays, we shall
see how much white space can be skipped over. Before we get to arrays,
which need more experience with pointers to handle to best advantage,
we'll look at some other ways in which scanf can be used, and at some
other aspects of pointers.

To start with, scanf allows a wide range of specifiers for its inputs, and
Fig. 7.5 shows the standard list, plus one optional extra. This does not,
however, reveal the splendid quirks of scanf. To start with, make the
scanf line in Fig. 7.4(a) read:

scanf("h%c",&p);

(not "%h%c", which is different) and try this version. If you simply
type a letter *which is not h* then what is printed out is garbage. If you type
a two-letter combination with h as the first letter, then the second letter

Note: In each case, the argument will be a pointer to the appropriate
type.

Mark	Meaning
%d	integer expected, denary number.
%i	integer expected in octal or hex.
%u	unsigned integer expected.
%o	octal number expected.
%c	character expected, field number indicates multiple.
%s	string expected, entry ends with space (whitespace).
%x	hexadecimal integer expected.
%h	short integer expected.
%e,f,g,E,G	float expected in appropriate format.
%%	expect % sign.

Zorland also contains:

%n	specification of number of characters.
%[	specify acceptable string characters (up to]).
%[^	specify string ending character (up to]).

Figure 7.5 The scanf specifiers, including some extensions in the Zorland
version of scanf.

will be correctly printed. In this example, the h is part of the specifier string, a kind of key which unlocks the action for you. Using %h rather than plain h implies a short integer, and you will have to find for yourself what this produces on your own compiler.

Now try using the specifier "%*c". This will produce only garbage, because the * symbol in a scanf line causes, as we have seen, the assignment to be skipped – you press a key but the ASCII character is not placed into the pointer address. Whatever happens to be in that address, whether from a previous assignment or (as in this example) by chance will then be used. I did say that the rules were strict.

Numbers again

One particular advantage of using scanf and printf together is the way that they can format numbers. Suppose, for example, that you wanted to knock up a quick program for inputting a denary number and getting the hexadecimal or octal equivalent. A lot of BASIC versions offer hex conversion nowadays, but octal is rather an oddity.

Figure 7.6 shows a conversion to hex, using scanf and printf. In the scanf line, the specifier "%5d" will allow a denary number of up to five figures to be used. If you use more than five figures, only the first five will be accepted. The output uses the "%x" specifier, which is the code for hexadecimal printing. The conversion isn't foolproof, because with x declared as an integer, its maximum entry is + 32767 denary, 0x7fff in hex. If you enter a number greater than this, then, the hex conversion lacks a leading digit. If this might be a problem, you might want to use a long integer or unsigned in your declaration, otherwise have a trapping statement between the scanf line and printf line. Now if you want to make this routine into an octal converter, all you have to do is to alter the specifier in the printf line so that it reads %o (oh, not zero), and also alter the message to read octal in place of hex.

```
main()
{
int x;
printf("\n Type a number...");
scanf("%5d",&x);
printf("Hex is %x",x);
}
```

Figure 7.6 A very simple denary to hex converter, illustrating the conversion facility of scanf and the hex printing ability of printf.

```
main()
{
int x,j,k;
k=0;
for (j=1; j<=5; j++)
  {
  printf("\n Number please (two digits max)");
  printf("\n%d ",scanf(" %2d",&x));
  /* scanf being used to return 1 */
  k+=x;
  }
printf("\n Total is %d",k);
}
```

Figure 7.7 A number totalling program which allows that scanf is a function which returns a number.

Another aspect of scanf is illustrated in Fig. 7.7. This program is a simple one for summing five numbers entered at the keyboard. To restrict the total to integer size, each number can use only two digits, and the sum is made by using the line:

   k + = x;

the shorthand version of k = k + x. The novelty in this program, however, is the use of scanf within a printf statement. This is not as odd as it might seem, though it's totally alien to BASIC thinking. What you must remember is that scanf is a function, and any function in C is likely to return *something*.

```
main()
{
int x,j,k,y;
k=y=0; /* initialize to zero */
for (j=1; j<=5; j++)
  {
  printf("\n Number please (two digits max)");
  y+=scanf(" %2d",&x);
  k+=x; /* count use of scanf */
  }
printf("\n Total is %d in %d entries",k,y);
}
```

Figure 7.8 Using the number returned by scanf to count the number of times that scanf has been called. Within a function, you would need a static variable for y.

As it happens, scanf is an integer function, so that it has an integer value which turns out to be 1 (the important point is that it is not zero unless something has gone wrong). By using a printf line with scanf embedded in it, we print this figure of 1 each time. This has nothing to do with the action of scanf and in this example it is simply a demonstration of a function returning a number, but it could be used, for example, if we wanted to count up how many times scanf had been used in a loop. Figure 7.8 shows this in action. The counting is pointless, of course, where a for loop is being used, but the principle is handy because, as we shall see in Chapter 8, there are loops which don't keep an automatic count of anything. In the example, the scanf statement is included as part of a piece of arithmetic. It's this ability to put functions in a part of other statements which provides a very sharp contrast between C and BASIC, and indeed between C and many other languages, and it is something that takes a lot of getting used to.

The way that pointers are allocated can also give some bother. In Fig. 7.4(b), the declaration char *p was used as a first step in a main program. What value this pointer p will take depends a lot on your compiler, and on most compilers will be any garbage number. You might get away with it; on the other hand this pointer might be an address in the piece of memory that holds the operating system. You can never make use of declarations of the type *p, *x and so on unless you do something to assign the pointer values (not what they contain, but the pointer addresses themselves). This could be done by having a variable previously declared, as in int y; *p;p = &y; which avoids problems by making pointer p equal to the address of the assigned variable y. At the instant when *p is declared, however, its value is taken virtually at random and it is only when the assignment p = &y is made that this becomes safe. Another safe way in which a declaration of *a, *b and so on can be made is within a function. If these quantities have values passed to them by the header of the function, then a suitable address will also be passed. For example, the function header:

```
safeone(xy)
int *x, *y;
```

presents no problems because the values of x and y are being passed through the header and will, we hope, be sensible values that already exist in the main program. This once again is a point (sorry) that is unexplained in most books, and you are left for yourself to puzzle out why an int *x, *y that works in one place causes havoc in another place. Once again, this is the kind of thing that gives C a bad name.

As an example of how correctly used pointers can be useful, take a look at the listing of Fig. 7.9. In this example, integers x and y are declared, and you are asked to input two numbers. The input uses a

```
main()
{
int x,y;
printf("\n Input two numbers");
scanf(" %d %d",&x,&y);
printf("\n x is %d and y is %d",x,y);
exchange(&x,&y); /* pass addresses, not values */
printf("\n now x is %d and y is %d",x,y);
}
exchange(a,b)
int *a,*b; /* must declare pointers */
{
int c;
printf("\naddresses are %u %u %u",a,b,&c);
c=*a;*a=*b;*b=c; /* swap objects pointed */
}
```

Figure 7.9 An exchange action, often contained in a library as swap, which works by re-assigning pointers.

scanf step; note the space ahead of each % step to allow for whitespace. This is particularly important for the second specifier because there has to be a whitespace separator between the numbers when they are entered. You can enter the numbers by typing one, then RETURN, then the other (and RETURN), or you can type a number, a space, the second number and then RETURN.

As usual, scanf requires the pointers to the integers, which are &x and &y. These will be sensible values because the integers x and y have been declared. The declaration of the integers prepares space in the memory, and that space has the addresses &x and &y. These pointer values are then assigned to a function exchange and the result will be to interchange the values of x and y as the last printf line reveals. The exchange function has in its header the quantities a and b which will contain the pointer addresses for x and y. These numbers a and b have to be declared in the pointer header, and since they are pointers to integers in this example, that is how they are declared.

In the body of the function, an integer c is declared. This could not be declared earlier because it's not part of the header, just a local variable. The next line then exchanges values. Variable c is assigned temporarily with the integer to which a points, in other words, x. The statement *a = *b means that whatever pointer a points to is changed so that it points to what b points to, in other words, a is made equal to b, so that both point to y. Next pointer b is arranged to point to the value in c, the old value of x. All of this leaves pointer a pointing at y and pointer b pointing at x. These numbers a and b, however, are the pointer addresses for x and y respectively that were passed to the function. Since &x now contains y and &y now contains x the values are swapped when you print them out. Note in particular the different types of quantities that we are working with here.

Quantities a and b are pointers to integers, and quantities *a, *b and c are integers. We can swap values of identical types, so that we can swap among *a, *b and c, and we can also swap between a and b, but we can't exchange with different types, such as *a and b without using a cast. This may seem odd when all of the quantities concerned are two-byte integers, but the division is important; we can make enough mistakes in C without any extra freedom, and if we *must* mix types we can use a cast. The printf line in the function shows the pointer addresses that have been used for a, b and &c respectivtly.

The important feature of this use of pointers is that it enables you to change variable values by means of a function. This is the only exception to the general rule that every variable declared in a function is local to that function. The use of pointers allows functions to pass back as many values as we need, rather than the limited ability of return which can pass back one value only. This is the type of use that makes pointers so valuable, and it accounts for the number of library functions which start with a header-full of pointer declarations. It's also the reason for scanf using pointer variables, because the purpose of scanf is to pass values into the main program or into another function, and to do so it simply has to make use of pointers.

8
Loops

The FOR loop

We have met the FOR type of loop briefly already, and in this section we shall simply summarise its syntax and action and add a few points that we have not considered earlier. To start with, the keyword for is followed by a set of three conditions. These conditions can be independent of each other, though for the most common applications of the for loop, the conditions all concern the same variable, a counter variable. The conditions are enclosed in brackets, and each condition is separated from its neighbours by semicolons, though see the note on the comma operator at the end of Chapter 6.

The first condition is an *initialisation*, and for the conventional counting loop it gives the initial value of the counting variable when the loop starts. This counting variable will have been declared and will normally be an integer or unsigned. The next condition is the *keep looping* condition, of the form of $x < = 5$. As we have seen it's important to form this condition correctly because looping will continue for as long as this while type of condition is true. The final condition is the *stepping* condition, usually the incrementing or decrementing of the variable. Normally we use something like $x++$ or $x--$, a simple increment or decrement, but we could use steps like $x*=2$, meaning that x will be doubled at each step, or $x-=3$ subtracting 3 from the value of x on each pass. The arrangement is therefore of an initialisation, a test and an action. These need not be on the same variable and need not even be connected though for most of the loops that we use the connection is that all three act on a single counter variable.

The for statement is one that *normally does not end with a semicolon*. There are two ways of marking the extent of the loop. One is to omit any semicolon until the end of the loop, and this can be used if there is only one statement line in the loop. The other method is to open a curly bracket in the next line following the for line, so that every statement between this and a closing curly bracket is executed as part of the loop, and such statements will all terminate with a semicolon in the usual way.

```
main()
{
char a;
for (a='a'; a<='z';a++)
printf("%c ",a);
}
```

Figure 8.1 Using a character variable as the controlling number in a for loop.

This latter method is preferable if the loop is being used for anything more extensive than a printf line.

As usual, C has surprises for the BASIC programmer. Take a look at the listing in Fig. 8.1, which shows a character variable being used in a loop. It's no surprise if you have programmed in PASCAL, but it's entirely foreign to BASIC. Once more, it's an example of the way in which C treats characters as ASCII numbers which, after all, is what they are. Note in particular how the character values are assigned, as 'a' and 'z'. This is something you have to be careful about, because if you use "a" or "z", things will go drastically wrong. The symbol 'a' means the character a, but "a" means two characters, the ASCII code for a followed by a zero. There will be much more of that when we get to strings in Chapter 9.

While we have a loop operating, we can take the chance to make some changes which will illustrate a few more points about how C uses loops. In particular, C has statements that allow you to skip passes through the loop, or to break out of the loop, without giving the computer's operating system apoplexy. BASIC is not nearly so well organised in this respect. Take a look at Fig. 8.2. The loop has been marked out with curly brackets this time, and to make it more readable I have indented this portion. In the brackets there is a new statement:

if(a == 'n')continue;

whose syntax and effect is rather interesting, to omit the letter 'n' from the printout! In this sense, 'continue' means continue the loop from the starting point (opening curly bracket) on, but it implies that anything that follows the continue statement in the loop will be left undone, and in the example, that means printing the letter 'n'. The syntax of continue will normally use an if test, and this is used in the way that is shown. The if keyword is followed by a test which must be enclosed in round brackets. As usual, the result of this test must be TRUE or FALSE, and another important point is the method of testing for equality.

Unlike BASIC, this uses two equality signs, or if you are testing for inequality, the ! = signs. You can, of course also use the < and > signs in this context. When whatever is enclosed in the bracket of the if test is

```
main()
{
char a;
for (a='a'; a<='z';a++)
  {
  if (a=='n') continue;
  printf("%c ",a);
  }
  /* loop enclosed in {} here */
}
```

Figure 8.2 Illustrating the use of continue to skip over part of a loop and return for the next pass.

TRUE then the continue action will be taken. What do you think would be the effect of using the condition:

if(a%2 == 0)

in the continue line? Try it, if you are in any doubt.

The continue statement is a way of excepting certain items (even-numbers, short names, one particular name) from being treated by the action of a loop. You can choose your position for the continue, too, because you might want to do some of the loop actions before you skipped the rest.

The other loop modifier is break. This, as you might expect, allows you to break out of the loop altogether as the result of some test. In the example of Fig. 8.3, it's when the value of character a reaches letter 'v', so that the loop prints out only as far as letter 'u'. In this example, of course, it makes little sense to do this, because we could just as easily have put this in as the ending condition at the start of the loop. You

```
main()
{
char a;
for (a='a'; a<='z';a++)
  {
  if (a=='v') break;
  printf("%c ",a);
  }
}
```

Figure 8.3 The action of break in a test to end a loop. After the break action, the next statement that will be run is the one following the end of the loop.

might, however, want to test for another condition, such as something non-numerical, in this way.

If your loop were, for example, reading a list of 100 names, you might possibly want to stop when you found McTavish, knowing that this name could be anywhere in the list. The continue and break actions of C avoid the messy and unpredictable effects of using GOTOs in BASIC loops, and the ability to use this type of loop with a character 'counter' opens up possibilities that don't exist in BASIC.

You can, incidentally, use a form of GOTO in standard C, though not all compilers support it. You need to mark each place that you need to jump to with a label word, followed by a colon. This label word can be in a line of its own preceding the routine that you want to jump to or at the start of such a line, like mark: x = 5;. The GOTO step then consists of a statement like goto mark;. Because of the provision of another two loop types along with continue and break, the goto action is hardly ever required, and if you think you need it, then you should consider rewriting your program.

While and do loops

The syntax of the while loop is simple and is used in several varieties of BASIC. The general form of a while loop is:

```
while (condition)
{
statments;
}
```

using the usual method of placing the statements(s) within the loop inside curly brackets. As before, however, if only one statement has to be executed, it can be followed by a semicolon to mark the end of the loop.

```
main()
{
char k;
k='a';
while (k!=3)  /* 3 is Ctrl C */
  {
  scanf("%c",&k);
  printf("%c",k);
  }
}
```

Figure 8.4 A simple while loop arranged to break on Ctrl-C – you would arrange for any key to be used for this purpose.

Also as before, the condition must be enclosed in round brackets, and must be something that can be evaluated as FALSE or TRUE. The loop will continue for as long as this condition returns TRUE.

Figure 8.4 illustrates a very simple type of while loop in action. One point to watch is that since a while loop makes its test at the start of the loop, whatever is tested will have to possess a suitable value at this point, otherwise the loop will not run at all. In this example, this has been done by assigning the value of 'a' to the character variable that is being used. The ending condition is for the character to be ASCII 3, the Ctrl–C combination of keys, and the reading and writing actions will continue in the loop until Ctrl–C is pressed – you do not have to press RETURN following Ctrl–C.

At this point, we can dispense with scanf for a time and look at the use of some of the functions that operate character by character. One such is getchar() which, as the name suggests, will get a character from the keyboard and which will require stdio.h in the #include line. The action is that the characters are obtained from the keyboard (the standard input) into a buffer until the RETURN key is pressed, but even that description does not quite prepare you for the action of the loop in Fig. 8.5(a). This is a typical condensed action line that you so often find in C programs, with a lot of activity poured into a few instructions. Because this is so

```
#include <stdio.h>
main()
{
char k;
while((k=getchar())!=9)putchar(k);
}
```
(a)

```
#include <stdio.h>
main()
{
char buf;
while (buf != 9)
   {
   read(0,&buf,1);
   write(1,&buf,1);
   }
}
```
(b)

Figure 8.5 Read and write actions. (a) The higher level functions for single character read and write are getchar and putchar, whose buffered action is not always desirable. You can use the low-level functions read and write instead (b), but not both on high and low level functions the same data.

unlike the structure (or lack of it) of BASIC, it will bear a long hard look, and we have to start inside the inner brackets at the statement k = getchar(). This is the normal way of using the getchar function, and its effect will be to get a character from the keyboard and assign this character to variable k, which has been declared as a character variable.

This getchar function tests the keyboard in a loop of its own, unlike the action of INKEY$ in BASIC, so that nothing happens until a key is pressed. The action also provides for echoing the character to the screen so that you can see what character you have typed. You can also delete the character with the delete key, because it is stored in a memory buffer until used by putchar.

The next level of brackets is used to enclose the test for a while loop. In this case, the test is for the character not being ASCII 9, the tab key character. The main action of the loop then follows in the form of putchar, a function that prints the characters from the getchar buffer. The net effect is that this program allows you to press keys and get characters on the screen. Pressing the RETURN key then puts the set of characters on to a new line (this is the putchar() action) and lets you start all over again until you press the Tab key. If you press the Tab key in the middle of a set of characters, then only the characters up to the Tab key are printed. If you run the program with the putchar statement removed, you will see the difference. The point here is that C combines into this very compact statement line the actions that in BASIC would need:

```
10 K$ = INKEY$
20 IF K$ = " " THEN 10
30 IF K$ = CHR$(9) THEN 60
40 PRINT K$;
50 GOTO 10
60 END
```

which is why C is the preferred language for systems programmers. These examples, incidentally, show that the descriptions of standard functions do not always prepare you for what the functions do, and in this case you might expect that the action would be to show each letter twice, side by side, as you typed.

The key to it is the buffer action of getchar, because this means that the loop does not run completely until the RETURN key is pressed. Until the RETURN key is pressed, the getchar action puts characters into the buffer, and the loop action with putchar will empty the buffer only after RETURN has been pressed. The presence of the Tab code in the buffer breaks the loop at that point. The use of a buffer for getchar follows the example of UNIX, but it's possible that some compilers may not have done this, so that the getchar action is terminated by the key that is pressed rather than by the RETURN key alone. In some ways this is

```
#include <stdio.h>
main()
{
char k;
while((k=getchar())!=9)
  {
   if(isalpha(k) && islower(k)) k=toupper(k);
   putchar(k);
  }
}
```

Figure 8.6 Adding some character function actions in a while loop.

more useful, and if the buffered method is used for getchar, then it's useful to have some other function that will allow the use of unbuffered input. If, for example, you have the getch() and the getche() functions available, try these in place of getchar() so that you can see the difference. Another possibility is the use of 'low-level' functions like read and write as illustrated in Fig. 8.5(b). You should, however, keep clear of such low-level functions unless you are very clear about how they work, which means familiarity with the MS–DOS system.

We can extend this to carry out rather more actions in the loop, as Fig. 8.6 shows. The while loop starts just as before, but there is no putchar action nor semicolon in the while line. Instead the start of the loop actions is marked by another curly bracket, and to make sure that you know this is the start of the loop I have indented the bracket. You don't *have* to do this, but it helps enormously in making your programs easy to read, for yourself as well as for others, and some compiler editors will automatically carry out this indenting when the program is written or when it is listed.

The first action is a test to find if the character is a letter. This is done by the isalpha(k) function from the library, which returns TRUE if the character assigned to variable k is a letter, FALSE otherwise. The other part of the test is done by islower(k), which will return TRUE if the character is a lower-case one. If both parts of this test give TRUE, then the character is a lower-case letter and the second part assigns k with the result of the function toupper(k) which converts from lower- to upper-case. Note how this assignment has to be done; you can't just use toupper(k) and then putchar(k) because carrying out the function toupper(k) does not change what has been assigned to k. That's one of the small points that will trip you up until you become really familiar with C. You can, of course, have statements such as:

    printf("%c",toupper(k));

that will print the result of the action of a function, but in this particular example, we want to alter the assignment to variable k and to do so needs the type of assignment that is shown.

As you would expect from the form of the test, this reassignment is carried out only if the character is a lower-case alphabetical character. The result is then printed by using putchar as before, and the closing curly bracket marks the end of the loop, with another curly bracket to mark the end of the program. When this one runs, the lower-case letters that you type are converted and shown as upper-case when you press RETURN, (use Tab to end the program).

```
#include <stdio.h>
main()
{
 char k;
 int d,m;
 d=0;m=1;
 while((k=getchar())!=10)
 /* end at RETURN key */
  {
   if(isdigit(k))
   {
    d=d+(k-'0')*m;
    m*=10;
   }
  }
 printf("%d",d);
}
```

Figure 8.7 A not very serious character to number converter. It might be useful if you like your numbers written backwards!

If you are getting quite confident, then perhaps it's as well to come down to earth by asking yourself what the program of Fig. 8.7 might do. The function isdigit(k) tests the character assigned to k to find if this is a digit, and will return TRUE if it is. We have declared variables d and m as integers and assigned to them starting values of 0 for d and 1 for m. If the character in k is a number, it is converted to number (integer) form by the use of (k – '0').

This is the shorthand C way of converting from the ASCII code version of a digit in k into the number that it represents, by subtracting the ASCII code for zero. The effect of this, then, is to convert the ASCII form of a digit into the digit itself. This is then multiplied by m and added to the existing value of d. Since d starts at 0 and m at 1, the result for the first digit will be to assign that digit's number to variable d. The next time round, this is added to ten times the number value, because the line m* = 10 has made variable m equal to 10, and on the next loop this will be 100 and so on. The net result of all this is to place the digits into a number variable that can be printed and used as a number. At the end of the loop, the printf statement prints out the result of all this.

Now try it. Type 123(Tab) and press RETURN, and the screen shows your 123 followed in the next line by 321! This is because the first digit that you type is being treated as the units digit, the next as the tens, and so on; the reverse of the way that we write numbers. If you type something like 12(RETURN) then 34(Tab)(RETURN) then the result is as you would expect from the first trial. If, however, you type something like 123(RETURN) 456(Tab)(RETURN) then the result is quite certainly not what you would expect.

By using so many digits you will have overflowed the size of an integer number, and this guarantees that the answer will be incorrect even if you entered the digits in order of significance. The moral here is that if you want to carry out conversions like this you need to use strings rather than the getchar action, or do the sensible thing and call up atoi. Knowing your library is a very important part of programming in C, because re-inventing the wheel is very time-consuming, and you might invent a lot of square wheels.

The do loop

The alternative to the while loop is the do loop, whose general syntax is:

```
do
    {statements
}while(test);
```

and as you can see, the test is made in the same way as for the while loop, but at the end of the loop. It's slightly unfortunate that the same word while has been used for both loops, because when you read a C program carelessly you can sometimes be trapped into thinking that the while is the start of a loop rather than the end. This can be avoided if you type your loops correctly indented so that the do and the while form an indented block, with curly brackets enclosing the statements. As it happens, the do . . . while loop is not used to nearly such an extent as the while loop. Nevertheless, it has its uses, most of which are bound up with the fact that the test of the loop is made at the end rather than at the beginning, like the REPEAT . . . UNTIL type of loop used in some versions of BASIC, though the test following while is the inverse of the test following UNTIL. If, for example, you want to create a 'Press the space-

```
#include <stdio.h>
main()
{
 char k;
  printf("\n Press spacebar to proceed...\n");
/* If \n does not follow phrase, the phrase is */
/* not printed. See what your compiler does */
  do
    {
     k=getch();
     }while (k!=32);
 printf("\nnext step");
}
```

Figure 8.8 Using a do loop for a 'Press spacebar' step which will ignore other keys. Zorland C follows UNIX methods, with the result that you must have a '\n' character, or use a fflush function, before a character input step like getch if a printing step preceded getch.

bar' step, the do loop is convenient, allowing keys other than the space-bar to be ignored.

The listing of Fig. 8.8 shows such a loop, including a function that might not have the same name on your compiler. This is getch() which tests the keyboard for one character only with no need to use the RETURN key; it's the equivalent of an INKEY$ loop in BASIC. This is an action that is very often needed, and you will almost certainly have either getch() or an equivalent on your own compiler package. The Zorland package contains both getch() which has no echo to the screen, and getche() which does.

The point of this example is that the loop has to be tested at the end since k has a value assigned to it by the getch function. Since the while form of loop is neater, it is used to a much greater extent except when the test is one that is applied to a variable that cannot be assigned with a value until later.

You can, of course, have as many steps as you want between the do part of a loop and the while test. Figure 8.9 shows an example of this in the form of a very simple integer to binary conversion. By very simple, I mean that this ignores things like negative sign, and is intended to work with numbers in the range 0 to 32767, the positive integer range.

The principle is that when an integer is divided by 2, it will give a remainder of 1 or 0 which forms one digit of the binary equivalent. The snag is that this process issues the binary digits in the order of least significant to most significant so that when the digits are printed they are in the wrong order, like the ASCII to integer example earlier. It is easy enough to reverse the order of a set of digits if they are in the form of a

```
#include <stdio.h>
main()
{
int n;
printf("\nPlease type an integer\n");
scanf("\n%d",&n);
itob(n);
}
itob(j)
int j;
{
printf("\n                ");
do
  {
   putchar(j%2+'0');
   putchar(8);putchar(8);
   j/=2;
   }
  while (j!=0);
}
```

Figure 8.9 An integer to binary converter, using left shift of the cursor to place the digits correctly.

string, but that's something we haven't looked at yet and we have to resort to trickery. In this case, the trickery is to print a space for the number, print the least significant digit, and then take two steps backward for the next digit. The backspace is obtained by using putchar(8), and the result is quite satisfying!

In the listing, the integer is obtained from the keyboard by using scanf, with the &n used because scanf always requires a pointer. If this were a serious program we would want to test the size of the number at this point, but for this brief example we simply call the conversion function itob(j). This uses printf to create a space of suitable size (sixteen spaces) and then starts a do...while loop that carries out the conversion. The action of putchar(j%2 + '0'); will find the remainder after dividing the number by 2, and convert this remainder, which must be 0 or 1, into ASCII code form by adding the ASCII code for zero. This leaves the value of j unaffected, and the next line carries out integer division to get a new value for j. The loop then continues until the value of j is zero.

After each character has been printed, however, the cursor is moved two spaces left by the two putchar(8) statements, so getting the digits of the number into the correct order. In this example, the items in the loop

102 *Simple C*

have been put between curly brackets and each statement is terminated
with a semicolon. There is no semicolon following do, and the while test
must be placed outside the curly brackets that enclose the loop actions.

Assortment

The while loop is one that, along with the for loop, you are likely to use
for most of the types of loops that you need, with the do loop being used
for just a few special cases. Every now and again, though, you will find
that there is a special requirement that doesn't fit neatly into these loop
arrangements. Usually this takes the form of a test that is part of the loop
and which cannot be part of the while test. The answer is almost every
example is the use of break or continue, sometimes both. The break and
continue actions can be put into any form of loop, and their use with the
while and do types greatly extends the uses of these loops. As an
example, Fig. 8.10 shows a simple character gathering program that
rejects any characters that are not letters and ends when a whitespace
character is found. This is an artificial example to some extent because
the whitespace character would be made part of the test in a while loop
but, as usual, it's an example intended to show actions, not to illustrate
neatness.

In this listing, the getch() function gets the ASCII code for key
character, and this is then tested. The first test is for the character being
whitespace (RETURN, Space or Tab) and this breaks the loop. The next
test is for the character not being a letter, and this causes the loop to continue back from this point. The use of continue at this point means that if
a digit or punctuation mark is typed, it will not reach the putchar part of

```
#include <stdio.h>
main()
{
char k;
do
 {
   k=getch();
   if (isspace(k)) break;
   if (! isalpha(k)) continue;
   putchar(k);
 }
 while(k);
}
```

Figure 8.10   A program that prints a set of characters that do not include
any digits, and which ends when a whitespace character is used.

the listing but will simply return to the start of the loop. Any character that passes both of these tests will get to the putchar statement and will cause the character to be printed on the screen. An action like this, incidentally, is not just a useless illustration, because it's sometimes important to be able to make a word that includes only letters with no whitespace or punctuation marks. One application might be for the entry of a filename or password, another is in the creation of artificial 'random' words for testing sorting programs.

9
Arrays, Strings and More Pointers

Arrays

In BASIC, you have simple variables, such as integers, reals and strings; and you also have one structured variable, the array. By 'structured', I mean that an array name like A means not just a single value, but a set of values which carry distinguishing names like A(1), A(2) and so on. C is very well equipped with 'structured' variables, or structured data types, as they are called. One of these types is the array and in this chapter we shall look at what it is and what we can achieve with it.

As you might expect, an array has to be declared at the start of a program and this declaration will include a name (the identifier), the number of elements in the array, and the type of data that is to be stored. This is just what you would expect from our experience of arrays in BASIC. When you use a DIM statement, such as DIM Name$(20), in BASIC, you are specifying the name Name, the type (string) and the number of elements (from 0 to 20, a total of 21). The main difference in C then will be the way in which an array is defined rather than the information which is used.

Suppose, for example, that we want an array called marks to hold a set of 20 integer numbers. The declaration that we need for this looks something like this:

    int marks[20];

This provides the name of the array, which is marks, the number of items (20 of them) and the fact that each item will be an integer. This variable declaration can be made along with other declarations of integers of the same line. One important point to note here is the use of the *square* brackets. If you forget that you are writing C and not BASIC, it's easy to refer to an item as marks(12), when you should be using marks[12] instead. The error message that you get when you do something like this will not necessarily remind you of what has gone wrong. Since the array in this example is an array of integers, you can use scanf to get each item of the array. One very important difference between the BASIC array and the C array, however, lies in the way that items are numbered.

When you define a BASIC array as A(20), then this allows for 21 items, A(0) to A(20). By contrast, the C array allows for just the 20 that you specified, and these will be [0] to [19], there will be no [20]. This might not stop you trying to use an item [20], and this is one of the things that you have to be very careful about, because C doesn't always stop you from doing foolish things, it lets you go ahead and pour garbage into the memory, which you don't find until later! Obviously, compilers vary, and some compilers might draw your attention to an obvious error, but in general mistakes like using an array item that has not been dimensional are run-time errors that the compiler does not catch. You must therefore test carefully and build in traps for this type of error because the memory corruption that something like this can cause will not point in any obvious way to the source of the trouble.

```
main()
{
  int num,marks[20];
  for(num=0;num<=19;num++)
    {
    printf("\nMark %d - ",num+1);
    scanf("%2d%c",&marks[num]);
    }
printf("\f\n%42s\n","MARKS");
for(num=0;num<=19;num++)
    {
    printf("\nItem %2d got %2d marks",num+1,marks[num]);
    }
}
```

Figure 9.1 Filling and printing a number array. Note what happens if a three-digit number is entered.

Figure 9.1 shows an example of this array in use, showing how the array can be filled and how its values can be printed with suitable formatting. In this program, a set of twenty integer numbers is obtained. These are assumed to be in the range 0 to 99, but there's nothing to stop you from entering numbers like 5000 unless you incorporate a loop that checks the numbers and calls for re-entry if an unsuitable value has been entered. The items are entered in a for loop, using principles that should be familiar by now. The prompt line uses num +1 rather than num so that you can use count numbers from 1 to 20 instead of 0 to 19. In the scanf line, the %2d allocates the numbers in twos. This is not ideal, because it means that if you type a four-figure number, it will be allocated to two sets of marks! For the moment, though, it will serve to keep the numbers below 99. The other point about the use of scanf here is that the array pointer is used directly, as &marks[num].

When all of the items have been entered, the screen clears, and the title MARKS is printed centred. This is done in the printf line by using the control string "\n%42s\n". The \n part takes a line down and the next part, the %42s, is a string *field size* number for the word MARKS. The field size number represents the total size of string that is printed, and if the word is less than this size, it is padded with blanks at the left-hand side (in other words, it is right justified). By using a positive number, we force the word to be printed with any of these padding blanks on the left-hand side. The choice of number 42 with MARKS (which has five letters) means that 37 spaces will be printed to the left of the name, leaving 38 spaces to the right of the name on an 80-character screen width.

The method of calculating the correct field size for centring a phrase is to count the number of characters in the phrase, add the number of characters per line for the screen width, and divide this total by two. If, incidentally, a negative field number is used, the excess spaces are printed to the right of the name. This can be useful for spacing the next name, but is not required for a single heading.

The items of array are then printed out in order, using the variable name num as the array number and num +1 as the item number. The printing line has made the spacing such that the lines will be uniform for both single-digit and two-digit numbers. This has, as usual, been done by using the specifier %2d in the printf line so that the field allows for two-digit numbers, and single digit numbers will be printed on the right-hand side of the field.

The method of using scanf with the number specified by %2d makes sure that no number of more than two digits can be entered. This is not always a desirable method of checking, however. The main problem is that if your finger slips and you enter 999 instead of 99, then 99 gets entered in one mark, and the last '9' becomes the first digit of the next mark. The program as it stands gives you no chance to do anything other than grin and bear it. This is a compiled program, remember, so you can't just use the old BASIC trick of commanding a GOTO to get you back into the right part of the program.

This method of specification, then, is suitable only when there is no loop involved, so that it doesn't matter if something gets left over. If you want to be able to correct an item without running the program all over again, then an IF test (as you would use in BASIC) is a preferable method, combined with a loop as shown in Fig. 9.2. In this listing, which is a modified part of the marks program, the assignment of scanf is to a variable tmp that will need to be declared in the earlier part of the program. The point here is that the value of tmp is tested in the do . . . while loop, and accepted only if the value is less than 100 (hard luck on swots).

```
main()
{
int num,tmp,marks[20];
for(num=0;num<=19;num++)
 {
do
 {
   printf("\nMark %d - ",num+1);
   scanf("%4d",&tmp);
 } while (tmp>=100); /* check size */
marks[num]=tmp; /* assign if correct */
 }
printf("\f\n%42s\n","MARKS");
for(num=0;num<=19;num++)
 {
 printf("\nItem %2d got %2d marks",num+1,marks[num]);
 }
}
```

Figure 9.2 Altering the routine so as to test for correct entry. The do loop will continue until a number less than 100 is entered, and only then is the array value assigned.

This is not quite so straightforward as it seems, because the scanf line has needed a change to %4d in its specifier in order to cope with the possibility of a number of up to four figures being entered in error. If this is not done, then you will still have the problem of a number like 999 being split into two. Note also that the logic of the while test is that the loop should continue if the entered number is 100 or more.

The golden rule is that your program should never bomb out when the unlucky user (you, perhaps) has just entered a lot of data, but this is never easy to achieve for every possible error. If, in this example, you enter a five-figure number as a mark, then it gets split among more than one array member as before. This is a scanf problem rather than one of program logic, and the answer is to enter numbers in string form and use a function to check and convert – but that's for when you have more experience. When you have written a number entry function like this, it's a good idea to add it to your library, because it's very likely that you will want to use it again without all the hassle of retyping it or re-inventing it.

Arrays and pointers

In the example of an array in use, we have stuck to methods that were not very different from the ways that an array is used in BASIC. Don't let this fool you, because the way in which an array is organised and the ways in which an array can be used in C can be startlingly different. The most obvious difference arises because of the way in which C uses

```
main()
{
int j,nr[5];
for (j=0;j<=4;j++)
 nr[j]=5-j;
for (j=0;j<=4;j++)
 {
  printf("\nItem %d is %d",j,nr[j]);
  printf("\nItem %d is %d",j,*(nr+j));
 }
}
```

Figure 9.3   Illustrating how the array values can be printed by using the array pointer for each value.

pointers. Take a look, for example at the short listing of Fig. 9.3 which fills a small array and then prints out the items in two different ways.

We needn't dwell on how the array is filled, or on how it is printed out by using nr[j], but the second printf line is certainly different. In this line, the quantity that is printed is *(nr + j), the content of the pointer addresses nr + j, and this gives exactly the same results as the quantity nr[j]. This is due to a piece of cunning (and economy) on the part of the designer of C in making the name of an array identical to a *pointer to the first member of the array.* When you declare nr[5], you are in effect creating address space for five integers (ten bytes), and the name nr is assigned with the address of the first item; in C language, nr is a pointer to the first item. To prove this, add the line:

   printf("\n%u",nr);

just before the end of the program and you will see the address number printed out when the program runs.

This address, then, is the pointer address for the start of the array, and if you have a machine-code monitor handy you can switch from your C compiler to the monitor so as to be able to look at this address and see what is stored in it. Whether you can do this or not, though, the point that is important is that the name of the array is itself a pointer, and we can get to any element of the array by adding the element number to the pointer name before using the * sign, as the example illustrates. This is something that we shall make more use of shortly when we come to consider the role of strings in C.

Multidimensional arrays

As in BASIC, arrays in C can have more than one dimension. As always,

this has to be declared, and the method of declaration is rather different
from the method that is used in most varieties of BASIC. Instead of
using a line like DIM A(5,4), for example, C uses the form int a[5][4],
using a separate pair of square brackets for each dimension number. The
items of the array are written in the same way, and the guiding principle
is that an array of this type is an *array of an array*. That apart, the use of
a multidimensional array is not so very greatly different from the use of
such an array in BASIC, as Fig. 9.4 illustrates.

```
main()
{
static int marklist[5][3]={
{56,47,62},
{81,65,56},
{74,54,67},
{38,52,46},
{63,50,48}
};
int j,k;
printf("\n%s%21s%20s%18s\n","No.","PHYSICS","CHEMISTRY","MATHS");
for (j=0;j<=4;j++)
  {
  printf("%d",j+1); /* number of item */
    for (k=0;k<=2;k++) /* marks in 3 columns */
      {
      printf("%20d",marklist[j][k]);
      }
    printf("\n");
    }
}
```

Figure 9.4 A two-dimensional number array in action. In this example, the
array is filled at the time of declaration and the numbers are then printed in
columns.

In this example, the array is dimensioned and filled in one operation.
This requires the use of a static array variable, and the form of the initialising is worth noting. Following the declaration is an equality sign and
an opening curly bracket. The numbers in the array are then listed,
separated by commas and held between the curly brackets. Following
each ending curly bracket is a comma until the last line has been filled.
The end of the initialising action is then marked by a final curly bracket
with a following semicolon. It takes a lot more space to describe than to
use. This initialising procedure is not, of course, something that can be
used only with two dimensional arrays, and any variable can be declared
and initialised in one operation, but the use of curly brackets and the
requirement for using a static variable is confined to arrays. The initialising of an array in this way takes the place of the READ . . . DATA lines
that are so beloved of BASIC programmers. In this example, of course,
the initialising has been done for the sake of example only, because in a
real-life program you would enter the data either from the keyboard or
from a disk file.

Following the declaration and initialising of the array, two more integer variables are declared to act as counters for the array printout. The rest of the routine is concerned with the printing of the array as a set of marks in different subjects for a group of five students. As is often the case, the arrangement of the printing is the really hard part of this program. The basis for the printing arrangement is the line that prints the marks in fields of 20 characters width. These fields start displaced by one character because of the line that prints the student number by itself at the start of each of the output loops. The aim on the long printf line is to get the subject titles positioned so that they will be reasonably centred on the columns of marks.

The best way of setting about this is a very old-fashioned method (hands up everyone who wrote FORTRAN programs on forms in the 60s) using layout paper. This is paper marked with 80 columns across the page so that you can position letters and numbers and see how they turn out. If you take such a sheet and write in a set of numbers using the correct columns then you can write in the title above them, correctly positioned, using pencil so that you can rub out and correct as required.

You can then count field spaces, remembering that this means the space from the previous last-printed character to the last character of the current word, and note these numbers for your %s specifiers. This has been done for the title line with the results shown for an 80-column screen, but you might prefer for some purposes to work with the PC's 40-column screen, in which case you have to use 40-column paper for planning. The two loops then print lines and columns of numbers, with the inner k loop responsible for the set of numbers in one line. Note that the numbering of j and k is, as always, from zero. The outer loop then moves from one line to the next, using a printf("\n"); statement to take a new line.

Finally, on this point, if you have strong nerves you can work directly with the array pointers. The substitution in the printing line is:

$$*(*(marklist+j)+k)$$

because the two-dimensional array is an array of an array. To get the first number of the set, for example, you need to use **marklist, and the line above gets the pointer stored in (marklist + j), adds k to this, and then uses this pointer to find the number.

Strings at last

A string in C can be regarded as an array of ASCII characters, ending with a zero. This is true in all versions of C, and even in some types of BASIC, but in BASIC there is a ready-made string variable type, marked with the dollar sign, as one of the main variable types. C does not have

```
#include <stdio.h>
main()
{
static char string[]="string test";
int n;
char *p;
p=string;
for (n=0;n<=11;n++)
    printf("\n%c, code %d is in %u",*(p+n),*(p+n),p+n);
printf("\n%s\n",string);
puts(string); /* simpler for unformatted string */
}
```

Figure 9.5 A string declared and initialised. The loop prints out the characters of the string to show that the ASCII codes are used, with a zero terminator.

these string variables ready-made, we have to define them for ourselves. A string is an array of characters, and we always define it in that way, as for example string[20]. When you write characters for a string in a program, you enclose them with quotes just as you would in BASIC, and you don't have to type in the zero that is always used to end the string. As an example, which is also a very important guide to the use of pointers, take a look at Fig. 9.5.

Now in this example, a string is assigned, and once again both declaration and assignment have been carrried out at the same time. This is possible only with a static variable in any variety of C, because C does not allow an auto array to be initialised at the time when it is declared. In addition, though, the number of characters in the string has not been declared, there is no number between the square brackets. This is something that can be done only in a combined declaration and assignment, and you can't split this into two statements like:

   char st[];
   st[] = "EXAMPLE";

The real meat of this example, however lies in the use of a pointer, defined as p. Now in the 6th line of the program, we make the assignment p = string, which looks very peculiar. It rather looks as if we are assigning a pointer, which is an address number, to the name for an array. You would expect by now that an assignment of this kind should be written as p = &st[0], and it would make not the slightest difference to the way that the program works if you did so. This is another of these short-cuts of C. The name of any array (and a few other compound data types, as we'll see) is the pointer address of the first item in array. The character array, like any other array, is stored in consecutive addresses in the memory, as this example shows, and the use of pointers is particu-

larly handy just because of that. You don't, of course, have to make use
of pointers if you just want to print a string or select one item from it.
You can print a string by using printf with a %s string specifier, as the
last line of the program shows, knowing that the pointer variable for the
string is the name of the string. You can pick a letter from the string by
using the fact that it is an array, so that string[4] is the fifth letter (the
count starts at 0, remember). Later, we'll see that it is possible to assign
and use a string using only the pointer, with no string variable name
directly used.

```
main()
{
static char string[]="set of letters";
printf("\n%s",string);
printf("\n Sixth letter is %c",string[5]);
}
```

Figure 9.6 Printing a complete string and selecting a character from a
string.

Figure 9.6 shows string selection more clearly. Once again the string is
initialised, and the complete string is printed using a printf line. Only the
array name, string needs to be used here, and no square brackets are
needed. In the following line, the fifth character in the string is printed
by using string[4] – remember once again that counting starts with zero.
Using the idea that each letter in an array can be located by using its subscript number, you can always assign one array to another variable
name. For example if you have string variables chars and string, both of
which are character array types, you can use a routine such as is shown in
Fig. 9.7 to make a copy of the array chars into the array name string.

```
main()
{
static char chars[]="Sample string";
char string[20];
int n;
for (n=0;n<=19;n++)
  string[n]=chars[n];
printf("\n String is %s",string);
}
```

Figure 9.7 Copying one string to another. This has been illustrated in the
main program to show the method, but would normally be carried out by the
strcpy function. The receiving string must be declared to a large enough
size.

This is pretty much the same method as you would use in BASIC to copy one array into another.

As it happens, you have a more efficient method available, in the form of the strcpy function in the library. Figure 9.8 shows the source code, and how this can be included into a routine – you would not normally type the source code for an established routine like this, but I want to show how the routine works. The library version makes use of pointers, as you might expect, and it's a good example of just how compact C code can be made, but unless you have the source code for your library you won't see how the function has been implemented there. Note in this version that the Zorland compiler warns about the line which looks like an assignment used in place of a test – as it happens the assignment is valid and correct here so the warning can be ignored.

```
char *strcpy(new,old)
char *new,*old;
{
static char *temp;
temp=new;
while (*temp++=*old++);
/* You might get a warning about that line */
return new;
}
main()
{
static char chars[]="Sample string";
char string[20];
strcpy(string,chars);
printf("\n String is %s",string);
}
```

Figure 9.8 The source code of the strcpy function, and how it is used in a program.

Let's get back to the strings, however. Figure 9.9 shows a very simple string variable reading and writing program. The word name is defined as an array of 20 items of type char. This means that name should not contain more than 20 characters (and this, remember, includes the terminating zero) but there is nothing to stop you from entering more than 20. A feature of C is that you have to build in your own safeguards – the language provides only the minimum necessary. If you enter only two characters from the keyboard, no harm is done, but the rest of the array will probably contain garbage which won't normally be noticed because any printout of a string stops at the terminating zero. If you enter 22

```
#include <stdio.h>
main()
{
 char name[20];
 int n=0;
 printf("\n Type a name, please\n");
 while((name[n++]=getche())!='\r');
 name[n]=0;
 n=0;
 while (name[n]!=0)
  putchar (name[n++]);
}
```

Figure 9.9   A string entry and print routine using getche. You would normally use a string entry function such as gets unless you needed to test characters individually.

characters, you may simply corrupt another string but, on the other hand, the program may crash at a later stage. After the declaration and initialisation steps, the program starts a loop with the line:

    while((name[n + +] = getche())! = '\r')

which is the kind of thing that gives C a bad reputation with academics. When you unravel it, it's not quite so bad as it looks, and you will soon learn to shrink lines down to this state for yourself. The way to unravel it is to start at the innermost brackets. Within these you find:

    name[n + +] = getche()

and this assigns the character from the keyboard (using getche()) to the array position name [n] and then increments variable n. Note that when getche() is used from my library, no buffer is involved and the RETURN key does not have to be pressed. This complete part of the statement is enclosed in brackets, following which is the ! = '\r' test to find if what is within the brackets is not equal to the RETURN key code. The whole of this in turn is enclosed in brackets which follow the while, and this has the effect of testing if the whole expression is TRUE or FALSE. If the key that has been pressed is not the RETURN key, then the expression is TRUE and the while loop continues.

  In other words, the character is put into the string and the place number is incremented. When the \r code is found, the expression that follows while is FALSE and that's the end of the loop. The whole of this while loop is in one line, marked by the semicolon at the end of the line. The two actions that follow are putting a zero at the end of the string, and then making variable n equal to zero again, Using name[n] = 0 actually causes the string to include \r character, but the effect of using name[n − 1] doesn't make much difference until the printout stage, when it changes the number of spaces under the printed version. We could, in fact, save a line here by using:

n = name[n] = 0

which carries out the two assignments to zero in one step. Finally, the putchar part of the work is done in two lines with another while loop, and you should be able to unravel that one for yourself from your experience of the putchar function. The whole of the input section can be carried out by the library function gets, however, and this is yet another reminder to look for such functions rather than roll your own – the home-made action here has been used to illustrate a point rather than as a serious suggestion for the input of strings.

In C, string actions look rather complicated because assignment is not quite so easy as you might think. Since a string is a form of array, and there's no method by which you can copy one array into another except character by character, it all looks like hard work. It's really only a problem, however, if you are 'thinking in BASIC'. You can assign a string constant, for example, by using #define in a lot of places where in BASIC you would use a string variable. You can also use the scheme of defining a static char string[] into which you can assign anything you want. You can also make a pointer point to any string you want, which is probably the easiest way of re-assigning a string name. We don't need to go into this, because it's one that exists in every C library.

You really need to use a string variable when you are inputting or outputting strings, and once again, there is a library routine, gets(string) for this purpose. We'll look at these routines later. The thing that you really have to be careful about is any attempt to assign a string to an array which is not large enough, because only a string of at least the same length is compatible. If your strings are arrays of 20 characters, then only another array of up to 20 characters total (including zero or any \n or \r character) can be assigned. This is very difficult to get used to when you have been accustomed to the free and easy ways that BASIC has with strings, and it's simply something that you have to come to terms with. the most important point for the ex-BASIC programmer, however, is to realise that a line such as:

string1 = "Example"

is almost invariably incorrect if string1 has been declared as a string array such as char string1[10] because it is impossible for string1 to be passed the address of "Example". This line will usually be caught by a compiler with the:

lvalue expected

error message, meaning that the left-hand portion is something that cannot be assigned to. On the other hand, if you declared in the form char *string1, the equation would be perfectly valid, because string1 is now an unassigned pointer, and the equation assigns the address of the word Example. The difference is that a pointer name is a variable, so that assignment to a pointer name is possible. The name of an array, though it acts as a pointer to an address, is a *constant*, not a variable, so that you cannot assign anything to it, it's a read-only pointer, if you like. This subtle difference causes all kinds of problems, and is seldom explained clearly even by seasoned C programmers.

Arrays of strings

In BASIC, you are accustomed to being able to use string arrays, with assignments such as A$(5) = "FRIDAY". In C, a string array is an array of an array of characters, another two-dimensional array with one of the dimensions being a set of ASCII codes. An easier method of thinking about it is to define a string as an array of characters, and then define another name as an array of strings. Once you have defined your 'string array' name correctly you can use the string array rather as you would in BASIC. You must remember, however, that the rules are rather more strict. Each name in the array, for example, will consist of not more than the declared number of characters, not forgetting the zero, and it's likely that anything following the zero that marks the end of a string will be garbage.

Look for example at Fig. 9.10. This consists of a program which will

```
#include <stdio.h>
main()
{
char name[10][20];
int n;
for (n=0;n<=9;n++)
   {
   printf("Please type name - ");
   gets(name[n]);
   }
printf("\n Names\n");
for (n=0;n<=9;n++)
 printf("\n%s",name[n]);
}
/* gets is ideal for this- you can run into */
/* problems trying character reading routines */
```

Figure 9.10 Entering and printing an array of strings.

fill an array with names (of up to 20 characters including the final zero), clear the screen, and then print the lot out. We start by defining name as an array of ten strings, each of which is an array of characters of up to 20 characters long. Two integers, n and j, are then defined to be used as counters. In the for loop, using n = 0 to n < = 9 because the array elements are 0 to 9, not 1 to 10, the array name is filled with names that you type from the keyboard, using the library function gets.

Each string is referred to by its two numbers, the place in the array of strings, and the character in each string. For example, name[2][4] means character 4 in string 2, remembering that character 4 is the fifth character, and string 2 is the third string. It's important to remember that you need two sets of square brackets here, unlike the BASIC method of using A(2,4). The zero is inserted automatically by the action of gets, so that you don't have to make any special provision other than dimensioning adequately. The array of strings is then printed on the screen by using the other loop. Each name in the array is obtained, once again, by using its position number with square brackets; name[7] in C is equivalent to NAME$(7) in BASIC. Note that this time, you *don't* have to use two sets of square brackets.

By specifying that you want to print a string, you have automatically made it unnecessary to specify the second set of square brackets. Just as you could use printf("%s",title); to print a string called title, which was defined as title[25], you can use printf along with the %s specifier to print a string which is called, for example, name[4].

A lot of BASIC programs depend on filling an array with values which are taken from an internal list. You might in BASIC, for example, want to fill an array WEEK$ with names taken from a DATA list of weekdays, such as:

```
20 FOR N = 1 TO 5
30 READ WEEK$(N):NEXT
```

so that any day can be found by use of the array number. These instructions are very wasteful of memory, because everything that you have in a DATA line in BASIC is stored in two places while the program is running. The action of READ . . . DATA in BASIC is really just the initialisation of an array in C, and the program of Fig. 9.11 illustrates this action in a form of a function which you can use for your own programs. This time, the array is an array of pointers, one pointer for each string, with no pre-declared restriction on string length because the length of each string is just the length of the quantity to which it is assigned. The name of the pointer array is week[], it points to a character type, and its initialisation is carried out as shown. The storage class must be static, if we are to carry out declaration and initialisation in one line, and the new feature is how a set of words, between quotes, can be put into an array.

```
main()
{
static char *week[]={
"Monday","Tuesday","Wednesday",
"Thursday","Friday","Saturday","Sunday"};
int n;
for(n=0;n<=6;n++)
 printf("\n Day %d is %s",n+1,week[n]);
}
```

Figure 9.11   A program that makes use of the array of pointers to strings that have been declared and initialised in one step.

The method is not so very different from that of Fig. 9.4 except that not so many curly brackets are needed for this array of pointers as for the two-dimensional array of numbers. The contents of the array are shown between curly brackets, separated by commas. In an initialisation, there is no need to show the number between the square brackets of the name, so this goes in as *week[]. When the array of strings is printed out, we don't print *week[0], *week[1] and so on, but week[0], week[1], etc. This is because the pointer name is the name of the array item. This is the kind of thing that's always likely to catch you out when you first start writing programs in C, and it's the first thing to suspect if you find that a printout gives you a screen full of gibberish.

Note, incidentally, that each string will end correctly with a zero. You haven't put this in, but it's taken for granted when you use letters between quotes, like "Monday". This is the important difference between using single quotes and double quotes. If you specify 'M', then a single character is stored. If you specify "M", then two characters are stored, the ASCII code for M and the terminating zero, because this latter "M"is a string.

So far, we have been looking at comparatively short programs. When your programs get to the length at which they take up more than one screen 'page', a printer becomes a more pressing necessity. It's particularly useful if you are using pointers and you are not sure whether you should be using a *x or just x at any particular time. If you can see the declarations at the same time as you look at the lines that are giving you the problems, it all becomes much easier. If your editor program supports windows that allow you to see more than one part of the screen, editing without a printer can be tolerable. Another problem is that by the nature of C, you tend to have a lot of nested { and } marks. If you can see these only on the screen, it's very difficult to be sure that each } corresponds to the correct {. Of course, if you planned the program correctly in the first place, you will have checked the nesting on paper.

The problem arises, however, when you have been doing some editing, repositioning lines, correcting mistakes and so on. At that stage, checking for an incorrectly placed } on the screen alone can be rather a frustrating task. One thing that can make a C program much easier to read is indenting each new { or loop. In this way, sections which are 'compound statements', running as if they consisted of one single instruction, are set away from the left-hand side in a block. This makes it easier to see where the { and } of each block is located. Another advantage mentioned earlier is that indenting makes it easier to see if a while is the start of a while loop or the end of a do . . . while loop.

More about pointers

We have made some use of pointers in programs and program functions, but the subject so far has really only been introduced. If you look through the routines in the source-code of your library (assuming that you have access to this), you will find that practically all of the standard routines make considerable use of pointers, rather more than we have done so far. The intelligent use of pointers can make a lot of apparently difficult program actions become relatively simple to achieve. A good reason for leaving detailed discussion of pointers until later in this book, however, is that the careless use of pointers can make a program unworkable. In many respects, the use of pointers in C is rather like the use of GOTO in BASIC – it can make a lot possible, but that can include a lot that you don't want.

Before we start on extended pointer exploration, then, recall for a few moments what a pointer is. A pointer is a number similar to an integer which locates a piece of data. A pointer can be defined as a pointer to an int, char or any other data type, simple or complex. If the data type is a simple one, the pointer is the number which gives the location of the first byte of that data. If the data type is complex, like an array or a structure, then the pointer gives the address of the start of the array or structure. If we want to make use of a pointer, we must declare its name, and also assign it. We can carry out actions on pointers that include incrementing and decrementing, addition and subtraction of integers, comparison of pointers, and the subtraction of one pointer from another (but only for pointers of the same type, and with unsigned numbers; you can expect curious results if you subtract a large pointer number from a smaller one).

The valuable feature of pointer arithmetic is that C makes automatic allowance for the size of data. If you have an array of characters, for example, then you can define and assign pc as a pointer to the first character. Incrementing this pointer, either by using + + or by adding 1, will get a pointer to the next character. Since each character takes up just one byte of memory, this isn't exactly surprising. If you have an array of integers, however, in which each integer uses two bytes of memory, then changing the pointer by using + + or by adding 1 will still get the next integer, even though the pointer has to change by two bytes this time. This is extremely valuable, because it means that you don't continually have to be worrying about the numbers that you add to pointers. You can, of course, add numbers greater than 1 if you want to get hold of other parts of an array.

```
#include <stdio.h>
main()
{
static char name[]="Ian Sinclair";
/* use your own name here*/
static int data[]={1956,1966,1983};
char *pc;
int *pn;
pc=name;
pn=data;
writit(pc);
dates(pn,3);
}
writit(p)
char *p;
{
 printf("\n");
 while(*p!='\0')
 putchar(*p++);
}
dates(p,n)
int *p,n;
{
 int j;
 for (j=1;j<=n;j++)
 printf("\n%d",*p++);
}
```

Figure 9.12 Passing pointers on to functions, showing the effects of incrementing pointers.

The use of pointers in this way, along with passing pointers to functions, is illustrated in Fig. 9.12. In this example, two arrays have been declared and initialised. One is an array of characters, the other is an array of integers. The assignments pc = nam and pn = data will make the pointers point to the start of each array. Note that this type of assignment is legal because the name of an array is also the value of its pointer. The important difference, you may recall, between the pointer that we assign and the name is that the name is a fixed (constant) pointer. In other words, we can assign pc = nam, because pc is a pointer variable, but we cannot assign nam = pc because nam is a fixed amount, the pointer for the start of an array, which cannot be altered except by assigning another array. Once the pointers have been assigned, we can use them in function calls. Two function calls are shown, one to writit(p) which will print a string of characters pointed to by p, and dates(p,n) which will print n dates, one on each line, pointed to by p.

The real meat of pointer use is now contained in the function definitions, and we'll look at writit first. This has been written simply to illustrate pointers, and you would normally use printf or puts for string printing. The header contains the parameter p which will have to be declared before the first curly bracket of the function, because this is the variable that is passed to the function. Since p points to a character, it is declared as such. Remember that these names are completely local to the function, we can change them without altering the quantities that are stored as pc, pn, n in the main program. Following the first curly bracket, the integer j is declared for the loop, and the loop uses putchar() to print a character on the screen.

The character that putchar uses is *p, the character that pointer p points to. At the start of the loop, p takes the same value as pc, because this was the value passed to it. In the putchar() statement, however, we use *p+ + so that the value of p is incremented by one character position after the character has been printed. This will ensure that the next character is fetched when the loop goes around again, and the while condition will ensure that the printing loop stops when the terminating zero of the string is found. The dates function behaves in a rather different way with an integer also passed to it, and printf used to ensure that the date is printed in the form of an integer number. Two variables have been declared in the header, and another, j is declared inside the function to be used as a loop counter. Once again, using *p+ + ensures the correct next number, though this time the memory is being incremented by two units instead of just one.

So far, so good. If you want to pass a pointer to a single integer or character, you must use the pointer-finding symbol &, which has been illustrated previously. This is particularly important when functions such as scanf are used. Generally, however, the main use of pointers is in connection with arrays because this is one of the ways that arrays can be manipulated as a whole.

As an example, take a look at the program in Fig. 9.13. This contains a function exchange which will swap two strings of different lengths, by swapping their pointers. Now it's important to realise that only the pointers are swapped, and the strings remain assigned to their original names. If we print out the string names before and after swapping, there will be no change. If we print out using the pointers, however, the swap will be obvious. The moral, then, is to work with pointers at all times if you are going to make such changes – if you want to swap the strings themselves, then use the routine shown earlier in Fig. 7.9. The routine declares and assigns two strings, name and city, and the pointers are declared and then assigned. The printf lines then show what the pointer addresses are.

```c
main()
{
static char name[]="Ian Sinclair";
static char city[]="Edinburgh";
char *pc,*pd;
pc=name;
pd=city;
printf("\n%u , %u",pc,pd);
printf("\n%s %s","Name is",pc);
printf("\n%s %s","City is",pd);
exchange(&pc,&pd);
printf("\n%u , %u",pc,pd);
printf("\n%s %s","Name is",pc);
printf("\n%s %s","City is",pd);
printf("\n%s %s","String name is",name);
printf("\n%s %s","String city is",city);
}
exchange(x,y)
int *x,*y;
{
 int tmp;
 tmp=*x;
 *x=*y;
 *y=tmp;
}
```

Figure 9.13 Pointers to pointers being used to swap pointers to strings. The strings themselves are not swapped, as the final printed lines show.

The first printing shows the pointer numbers and the names in the correct order. Following the exchange function, however, the pointer

numbers are swapped, so exchanging what they point to. This appears
only if we print the pointers pc, pd, not the names nam and town which
do not change. Note that the printf line uses pc,pd and not *pc,*pd.
Once again, this is because the name of an array is the pointer to its starting address. In this context, quantities such as *pc,*pd are meaningless
unless you want to see the first character of each string, which is all that
you get.

The pointer exchange is carried out using pointers to the pointers. The
pointers to the strings are simply two numbers which are stored in the
memory. To exchange them in a function, we needd to find where these
pointer numbers are, and we can do this by finding their own pointers.
This is done by calling function exchange with parameters &pc, &pd,
which are the pointers to pc, pd respectively. These pointers are passed to
the function as numbers x and y, and defined as pointers to integers,
which they are. The integers that they are pointing to are the pointers
pc,pd. We then use these pointers to exchange the values of pc and pd.
We cannot simply exchange pc and pd in a function, because the
function works with local values only. At the end of the function, any
quantities that are passed to the function are restored to normal.

If we work with pointers, however, we can make permanent alterations in anything that these pointers point to. In this case, the quantities
that we are working with are temporary values x and y. These are manipulated so as to exchange pc and pd, pointers which have not been
directly passed to the function. Using pointers in this indirect way is the
only method by which a function can make changes in a number of parameters. The routine carries out the swap, and when the main program
takes over again, you can see that the pointers have been swapped. The
important feature here is that a pointer is a two-byte number. You can
swap pointers like this around as much as you like, and the action is
quick and easy. It's certainly not so easy, and definitely not so fast to try
to swap the actual contents of strings around. You wouldn't be advised
to try it on strings of unequal defined lengths, either, but when you work
with pointers all things are possible. If, incidentally, you want to find
where the pointers to the pointers are stored, add a line:

    printf("\n%u,%u",x,y);

just following the int tmp declaration in the function.

Arrays of pointers

An array of pointers is a method of locating data which is often more
useful than other types of arrays. It would be rather pointless (sorry!) to
use an array of pointers to integers, because it's simpler to use an array of
integers, and it would take less space. Arrays of pointers come into their

124 Simple C

own when they are used to refer to arrays of arrays. An array of strings, for example, consists of an array of arrays of characters. A useful alternative to a string array formed in the way that we have used previously, then, is an array of pointers to strings. As we have seen, this allows for actions such as exchanging to be carried out.

To form and make use of such an array of pointers we have to know what syntax has to be used to refer to pointer arrays. Figure 9.14 shows a pointer array being used to swap pointers around so that the string arrangement is different, using a simple swap routine for three items rather than the complications of a full-scale sort routine for so few items. Note that, contrary to what you might expect, you have to use the address sign, & in front of the pointer array values in order to pass the pointers to the pointer values correctly to the function. Another point to note is that the use of a function will successfully result in obtaining pointers to the pointers, but this is not so simple if you want to carry it out in the main part of the program. The reason is that quantities such as

```
main()
{
static char s1[]="Zero value";
static char s2[]="Absent value";
static char s3[]="Middle value";
char *ptr[3];
int p,j;
ptr[0]=s1;ptr[1]=s2;ptr[2]=s3;
for (j=0;j<=2;j++)
 printf("\n%s",ptr[j]);
 printf("\n");
alter(&ptr[0],&ptr[1],&ptr[2]);
for (j=0;j<=2;j++)
 printf("\n%s",ptr[j]);
}
alter(x,y,z)
int *x,*y,*z;
{
 int tmp;
 tmp=*x;
 *x=*y;
 *y=*z;
 *z=tmp;
}
```

Figure 9.14 Altering the order of strings in a pointer array.

ptr[0] are defined as string pointers and you can't obtain pointers to them in any straightfoward way.

The only simple assignment you are allowed to make is of another pointer to a string. You can get around this restriction by using a cast, something that is very poorly illustrated in most books on C. The use of cast is to make a quantity become of a specified type, and the syntax is (type)quantity. This doesn't illustrate how cast is used, however, quite so dramatically as Fig. 9.15. In this example, the strings have been printed in quite a different way that illustrates the usefulness of pointers to pointers. The line:

    s = &((int) ptr[0]);

will have the effect of making the quantity ptr[0] temporarily into an integer, and then taking the address of this integer and assigning it to integer pointer s. Using the correct cast expression allows s to carry the address of ptr[0], and the printing loop can now make use of *s + + both to print the value and to increment to the next string. This is simple because the string pointers are held at consecutive addresses – the print-out shows the pointer addresses for both pointers and data.

Another aspect of the use of pointers with string lists is how easily an item can be located. This makes for very efficient and short routines for such actions as finding the day of the week from a number. An illustration of this use is shown in Fig. 9.16, which starts with the definition of a

```
main()
{
static char s1[]="Zero value";
static char s2[]="Absent value";
static char s3[]="Middle value";
char *ptr[3];
static int p,*s;
int j;
ptr[0]=s1;
ptr[1]=s2;
ptr[2]=s3;
s=&((int) ptr[0]);
for (j=0; j<=2; j++)
  {
  printf("\n%u , %u",s,*s);
  printf("\n%s",*s++);
  }
}
```

Figure 9.15 Using a cast to convert a pointer into an integer.

function. The function is of type char and it will return a pointer, because this is what the name of one item will be, one of the array of pointers. The header will put in an integer which will consist of a number in the range 0 to 9. A number such as 10 will count as 1, because only the first character will be accepted by the main program call to getchar. For a more serious program, you would read the number with gets, convert with atoi, then loop around until the number was in the correct range. This number is declared and treated as an integer in the function, and the pointer array *day is declared and (since it is static) assigned. The assignment of the zero position is made to a message. After this, the last line of the function returns the selected string. The variable c is used as a selector in the line

return((c < 1||c > 7)?day[0]:day[c]);

so that if c is less than 1 or more than 7, the string day[0] will be returned, giving the message 'no such day'. For numbers between 1 and 7 inclusive, the correct day of the week is returned, counting Monday as day 1. The 'no such day' message is returned for number 0,8 and 9, but if you type 10, then you will get Monday because only the 1 of the 10 has been accepted by getchar(). There is an old programmers' proverb that a fool can make more mistakes than a wise programmer can ever anticipate. There is also a users' proverb that states that a programmer can make more mistakes than anyone can anticipate.

```
#include <stdio.h>
char *getname(c)
int c;
{
 static char *day[]={
"no such day","Monday","Tuesday",
"Wednesday","Thursday","Friday",
"Saturday","Sunday"};
return((c<1!!c>7)?day[0]:day[c]);
}
main()
{
char c;
printf("\n");
printf("\n Day number please-   ");
c=(getchar()-48);
printf("\n%s",getname(c));
}
```

Figure 9.16   A day number to name converter using pointers.

10
Menus, Choices and Files

Most varieties of BASIC allow a neat and simple method of programming menus, using the ON K% GOSUB type of command. Since a
menu is a very common feature of a lot of programs, it's time that we
took a look at how such a system can be programmed in C. The key to
simple menu programming is the switch statement, which is the C equivalent of ON K% GOSUB. Suppose that you have a list of items on your
menu, with each item numbered in the usual way. You then use a keyboard read function to input a number. Suppose, for example, that you
use the getchar function, you can then program:

```
switch(getchar() – 48)
{
    case 0:(first action);
    break;
      case 1:(second action);
      break;
```

and so on, with the closing curly bracket at the end of the list. The function getchar() will have values which are ASCII codes for numbers such
as 0,1,2, and so on, so that getchar() – 48 converts to number form as we
saw earlier. You can, of course, use getche() or other input functions as
you please, depending on whether or not you want to press RETURN to
get the value. The entry of the number allows switch to select the
command which appears after the same number in the list that follows
case. You could equally easily omit the conversion and use lines like case
49, but this is undesirable because compilers generally will allocate space
for the missing cases 0 to 48, so wasting space.

In a real program, each of these options would consist of a function
name, or a statement, and there would be some form of error-trapping to
ensure that the correct range of number choices was not violated. For an
illustration, we can substitute simple printf statements, as in Fig. 10.1.
The important point is to understand why the break statement has been
added in each line.

```
#include <stdio.h>
main()
{
int j;
printf("\n%42s\n","MENU");
printf("\n%10s","1. Start new file.");
printf("\n%10s","2. Add items to file.");
printf("\n%10s","3. Delete item.");
printf("\n%10s","4. Change item.");
printf("\n%10s\n","5. End program.");
printf("\n%10s  ","Please select by number- ");
printf("\n"); /* last printf get into do loop! */
do
 {
 switch (j=getche()-48)
  {
   case 1:printf("\n start new file");
   break;
   case 2:printf("\n add to file");
   break;
   case 3:printf("\n delete item");
   break;
   case 4:printf("\n amend item");
   break;
   case 5:printf("\n end of program");
   break;
   default:printf("\n No such item- %d please try again.\n",j);
  }
 }
 while (j>5||j<1);
}
```

Figure 10.1 An example of menu construction using switch and case. Note the importance of the break statements.

In the example, a title is printed and the fielding command %42s has been used. Note that when anything like this is done, the message must be separated by a comma from the fielding. If you use:

   printf("%42s\n MENU");

you will probably see a set of gibberish characters appear preceding the word MENU, though compilers differ and you may find that yours permits this. The menu items are then printed, with a number allocated to each item. Notice the use of "%10s", the C equivalent of TAB(10). You are asked to choose by number, and a large do loop starts.

The first loop action is to obtain the number choice, using getche() in the usual way. This, however, appears as the second part of the switch statement, showing once again how C can make these very useful compound statements for a set of actions that would require several lines of conventional BASIC. The switch statement is then followed by a list of choices, each of which starts with the keyword case followed by a number. Each number is followed by a colon, then the action or actions that must be carried out. The set of switch actions must end with a closing curly bracket, and the whole program ends as usual with the final curly bracket. Each choice has simply caused a phrase to be printed in this example, because the aim is just to show what the switch statement does and how it is programmed.

To see why we need the break statements, try omitting one or two. You'll see that this has the effect of allowing more than one answer to be printed. The switch statement allows you to select one item, but when the action returns, it will move to the next case statement. Unless you want the next case line to be carried out, you must make this next statement the break to allow the rest of the switch sections to be skipped. Notice, too, that we can cater for a selection which is not in the range that switch allows. This is done by the default item, and it's a very handy way of ensuring that the entry range is checked and something sensible done for each possible answer.

Since all this is enclosed in a do . . . while loop, the selection is repeated until a choice in the correct range is made. The message is printed by the function, and the do loop along with the default statement ensures that the choice can be made again until the number lies in the correct range. It's not quite so straightforward as it seems, however, If you simply add a do . . . while loop to an existing menu, you need a quantity to test at the end, and this can be obtained by using a variable to store the value obtained from getche. In the example of Fig. 10.1, the integer j has been used, and the while test contains:

$(j > 5 \| j < 1)$

with the vertical bar signs used to mean logical OR, so that the statement in brackets tests the truth of 'j greater than five or j less than 1'.

Other cases

The control for switch does not have to be defined as an integer because, as we have seen previously, a character is entered as an ASCII code which is a single-byte form of integer anyhow. You can, therefore, use a character to control a switch, as is illustrated in Fig. 10.2. In this example, the variable s is of type char, meaning a letter, and the switch statements are set up for letter testing. We can still use s = getche() to get the character from the keyboard, however. This is because, once again, the language does not make any rigid division between characters and integers – the main difference as far as the computer is concerned is that a character is stored in only one byte of memory, and an integer requires two bytes. Note that a character is referred to by using its key, within single quotes, such as 'S', 'A' and so on. This is something you constantly have to remember, because using double quotes, such as "S", "A", means a

130 *Simple C*

string which consists of the letter code and a zero. An alternative, not seen so much nowadays, is to use the backslash with the *octal* version of the number, like \101 you can also use a *hex* number in the form \x41. As it stands, the program does not discriminate between a consonant, a digit and a punctuation mark. This type of character input can be improved by using some of the built-in library functions. The improved program is shown in Fig. 10.3. This time, the test for escaping from the loop (the @ character) is made at the start, using a while loop. You have to be careful how this is done, with the s = getche() step enclosed in brackets and made not equal to '@', and the whole expression in brackets for the while statement. If you get these brackets wrong, such as by using:

    while(s = getche()! = '@')

then you will find that s will be assigned with either 0 or 1, depending on whether the key that was pressed was @ or not respectively. The inner brackets in the listing are essential to ensure that s is assigned with the character rather then with the 0 or 1 which is the result of the test using ! = . By putting this test in the outer brackets you make it apply to the while loop rather than to the assignment. In the loop, two tests are then

```
#include <stdio.h>
main()
{
char s=' '; /* spacebar used */
do
 {
  printf("\n type a letter (@ to stop)\n");
  if (s!='@')s=getche();
  switch(s)
  {
   case 'a':
   case 'e':
   case 'i':
   case 'o':
   case 'u':printf(" - is a vowel\n");
   break;
   default:printf("  -is a consonant\n");
  }
 }
 while (s!='@');
}
```

Figure 10.2 Controlling the switch action with a character variable.

```
#include <stdio.h>
main()
{
char s;
  printf("\n type a letter (@ to stop)\n");
 while((s=getche())!='@')
 {
 if (isspace(s)) continue;
 if (!isalpha(s))
 {
  printf(" not a letter \n");
  continue;
 }
 tolower(s);
  switch(s)
  {
   case 'a':
   case 'e':
   case 'i':
   case 'o':
   case 'u':printf(" - is a vowel\n");
   break;
   default:printf("  -is a consonant\n");
  }
 }
}
```

Figure 10.3 An improved character testing program, using some of the is set of character testing functions along with tolower.

made. The first test uses the isspace function, which is TRUE if so happens to be a space, the newline character or a Tab. In this example, it's the newline we are trapping, and the effect will be to continue if the character is a newline.

The continue statement used in any type of loop means that the rest of the loop will be skipped, and the loop is restarted. If the newline is found, then, the loop returns for another getchar. The next test uses function isalpha. By using this in the form:

    if (! isalpha(s))

we get a TRUE answer if the character is not alphabetical. For this event, we print out the 'not a letter' message, and continue to get another letter.

If character s has survived so far, we then use function tolower(s) so that any upper-case letter is converted to lower-case. This avoids the problem of entering an upper-case letter like A, E, I, O, U and being told that each is a consonant. All of these functions will be in your library, and on the Zorland compiler you should use the ctype.h header along with most of these functions, though the program illustrated here compiled with no problems under the Zorland compiler/linker.

One last point about switch is well worth mentioning if you have been used to writing BASIC programs that make selections from strings entered at the keyboard. The expression that follows switch, within brackets, must give a single integer. You can't for example, make switch work with strings, except to recognise the first character of a string. If you have to work with strings, then a program like the one in Fig. 10.4 will be more suitable.

```
#include <stdio.h>
main()
{
int n;
char command[6];
printf("\n Please type command");
printf("\n cls,dir,date,time,Q(uit)\n");
do{
    gets(command);
      if (!strcmp(command,"cls"))system("cls");
      if (!strcmp(command,"dir"))system("dir");
      if (!strcmp(command,"date"))system("date");
      if (!strcmp(command,"time"))system("time");
    } while(strcmp(command,"Q"));
 }
/* Note that to use system commands you need to have */
/* COMMAND.COM available on Zorland C                */
```

Figure 10.4 Menu action with strings. The switch action cannot be used unless one character is extracted (like Cls, Dir,dAte,Time) to be used.

The name command is defined as a string of up to six letters, and it is filled with characters inside the do loop by using the string input function gets. The word that is obtained as command is then compared with a list of 'keywords' by using if tests along with strcmp. Remember that there is no way in which you can compare one string with another directly in C, so that lines such as:

   if(command == "cls")

are *never* valid, and will produce the '1value expected' message. This is something that takes a long time to get used to if your programming experience has been in BASIC or even in PASCAL. The strcmp

```
#include <stdio.h>
main()
{
int n,a[51];
FILE *fp;
for (n=0;n<=50;n++)
 {
 a[n]=2*n;
 }
printf("\n array is now filled ");
fp=fopen("intfil","w");
for (n=0;n<=50;n++)
 {
 fprintf(fp,"%5d\n",a[n]);
 }
fclose(fp);
}
```

Figure 10.5 Disk filing for an array of integers.

function, which is in the function library, does the comparison character by character, and returns a number whenever two characters are unequal. If the strings match perfectly, then the function returns 0. We therefore have to test for NOT strcmp, therefore, using the ! sign.

In this example, the standard strcmp function has been used, so that the program example will do MS-DOS things like clear the screen, list the directory, alter time and date by using commands such as cls, dir, date and time. The important points are that the words do not necessarily need to appear on screen (though they do here because of the use of gets), and that the comparison can be made. You will need to press the Q key to get out of this one, because the while condition will make it loop until this key is pressed.

Data files

Once you have made a start to gathering information into arrays, then it's likely that you'll want to record the information on to disk. We'll start at the beginning, and look at what is involved in recording and replaying a list of integers which will be held in the computer as an array. Figure 10.5 shows what is involved. The integers are generated in a loop, which simply gives all the multiples of two up to 100. Once this array has been generated, the recording file is opened by using the line:

    fp = fopen("intfil","w");

in which fp is a pointer to the start of the file, "intfil" is a filename that
will be used on the disk, and "w" means write. Note that this is "w", a
string, not 'w', a character. Some compilers will accept the definition
int *fp but the much more common declaration as used by Zorland is
FILE *fp, and FILE is defined as a structure in the stdio.h header. Once
the file has been opened, the array can be recorded by using another
loop, with a variation on printf being used in the writing process. The
function fprintf is used very much like printf, but with the file-pointer as
the first of its arguments.

Specifier	Use
"r"	Read file only.
"w"	Write file, overwrite any file of same name.
"a"	Append to existing file, or start new file.
"r+"	Open for reading and writing.
"w+"	Open for reading and writing, overwrite existing.
"a+"	Open for reading and writing with appending.

Use of b following any of these (within quotes) specifies a binary
file as compared to the normal text file.

Figure 10.6   The use of the mode specifiers in opening files. Note that
these mode letters are strings, not single characters.

The whole action could have been carried out in one loop, but I
wanted to separate the generation of the numbers from the filing routine
so that it would be easier to adapt the program for something more
useful. The file must be closed by using fclose(fp) after writing. If there
has been any other file called intfil on the disk, it will be deleted by this
action. Figure 10.6 shows how Zorland C uses the letters "r", "w" and
"a" in these file commands. In general, your compiler will give you the
choice of reading, writing or both, and the further writing choice of
overwriting a file of the same name or appending more data to it.

Once the (serial) file is on disk, you can look at it, after a fashion, with
the TYPE command of MS-DOS. This involves leaving the C compiler
temporarily to switch into DOS, and typing TYPE intfil. You will see the
integers appear, very untidily, on the screen with a newline for each new
integer. This shows that integer numbers are recorded in string form
rather than in the coded two-byte form in which they are stored in the
memory. To read the integers back in a more controlled way, we should
write a reading program in C – and that's the next step.

One possible reading program is illustrated in Fig. 10.7. This one
prepares in the usual way, and opens the file using:

```
#include <stdio.h>
main()
{
int n,b[51];
FILE *fp;
fp=fopen("intfil","r");
for (n=0;n<=50;n++)
 {
 fscanf(fp,"%d\n",b+n);
 }
fclose(fp);
for (n=0;n<=50;n++)
 printf("%d ",b[n]);
}
```

Figure 10.7 Reading the file of integers that was prepared by the preceding program.

    fp = fopen("intfil","r")

with the "r" (not 'r') meaning "read" in this case. The loop is performed as before, but this time fscanf is used, and the syntax is not the same as that for fprintf. The reason is that an array is being filled, and fscanf needs a pointer to the position in the array. Now the name of the array, b is the pointer to its first item, b[0], so that if we use b by itself in the scanf instruction, all numbers will be read into the first item. To make the pointer shift to the correct item, we use b + n, so that the correct number of address bytes beyond the pointer start b will be used. Remember that when you add to a pointer in this way, the number that is actually added is a calculated number, taking into account the type of data. For example, an integer uses two bytes. If pointer b happens to be 9600, for example for n = 0, then for n = 1, the address is 9602, because an integer takes two bytes. This automatic adjustment is very useful, but easily forgotten.

After the numbers have been read, the file is closed in the usual way, and the array is then printed out. The printout is not in the same format as was used for reading the array in, which is the main benefit of using a separate loop for this purpose.

The use of fprintf and fscanf is just one of a set of ways of using disk filing. Figure 10.8 demonstrates two other functions which can be used putc() and getc(). As the names tell you, these are character functions, but this description can be very misleading, particularly as applied to getc(). The action of getc() is to return an integer, which can, of course, be regarded as a character in ASCII code. The important point is that you can assign getc() as an integer or directly as a character, but it's better *always* to assign it as an integer. The reason is that you generally use getc() in a loop which continues until the end-of-file character is found.

```
/* you might need to use #define EOF -1 */
/* unless your #include <stdio.h> does this *.
#include <stdio.h>
main()
{
char a[51];
int n,j;
FILE *fp;
n=0;
fp=fopen("newchar","w");
while ((n<=50)&& ((j=getche())!='0'))
 {
 putc(j,fp);
 n++;
}
fclose(fp);
printf("\n press RETURN key to read file");
getchar();
fp=fopen("newchar","r");
if (fp==0)
 printf("\n no such file");
 else
 while ((j=getc(fp))!=EOF)
  {
printf("%c",j);
   a[n++]=j;
   }
 a[n]='\0';
 fclose(fp);
 printf("\n%s",a);
}
```

Figure 10.8   Using the putc and getc functions in a file program.

The EOF character in C is −1, which is integer form consists of two bytes, hex FFFF or denary 65535. If you read getc() as a character, it will only deliver one byte, and the end of file character cannot be read. That's usually one fruitful cause of program crashes. Another one is to gather the characters into a string and forget that there must be a zero at the end when the string is printed. One rueful programmer said that C was the shortest road from a keyboard to a bug and there are times when we all feel that way.

Looking at the program of Fig. 10.8, then, the assignments are made as usual with character string a, and the others integers. As before, the pointer has been defined as a pointer to an integer. The counter n is initialised to zero so as to make a count of the maximum number of characters that can be entered.

The file is opened, and a while loop starts. In this loop, the number of characters that can be entered is limited to 51 (from 0 to 50), and the loop condition also includes a getche() step that will allow entry of a character and detect a zero being pressed. This allows you to type letters as you please, using spaces, newlines or whatever, until the zero key is pressed. The file which was opened at the start of the program is then used by putc(j,fp) to place the character corresponding to integer j in the file which is pointed to by fp. This loop continues until a '0' is entered or until the maximum permitted number of characters has been entered. The file is then closed, and the program hangs up, waiting for you to press the RETURN key.

When you press RETURN, the program then continues, opening the file for reading. Now it can happen that you do not have the correct disk in the drive when you are reading a file, and the next part of the program shows how to deal with this contingency. The pointer fp will be zero if no file exists, so that testing for (fp == 0) allows you to print a message. In a real program, of course, you would want to return to the waiting step if the disk turned out to be the incorrect one, but in this example, the program simply stops if the newchr file is not on the disk. If the file is found, then a while loop reads it until the EOF character is found. The EOF has been defined in the stdio.h header as − 1, the correct EOF for C; it is very unlikely that your compiler will differ in this respect.

We could, of course, have used − 1 in place of EOF, but if you use EOF and #define, or read in the EOF definition in a #include file like < stdio.h >, it's much easier to change a program so as to run on another machine (or another variety of C). The getc() function is assigned to the integer j so that the EOF can be detected, and the conversion to characters is done simply by using a[n++] = j, in which the character is placed in the array of characters and the place number incremented. When the loop ends because of the EOF character, the '\0' is added to make the array into a true string. The file is closed, and the string of characters is printed (not the final 0). Now you can start condensing the size of the program by merging actions in the usual C way.

String files

The use of number files is seldom particularly important, except as parts of other files. That's something that we shall take a close look at in Chapter 11. Character files, however, are the stuff of editors and word processors, and the extensive involvement of C in such activities shows in the number of library functions that deal with character recognition and testing. For the moment, though, we want to look at the important string file. As you know, a string in C is an array of characters which ends with a '\0' marker. An array of strings can be dealt with in two ways. One is as an array that has two dimensions, such as a[10][10], another is by keeping an array of pointers. Experienced C programmers work as a matter of preference with pointers, and we have already had a taste of this when we saw that a pointer plus a subscript number could be used to refer to an item in an array. In the following example, we'll make much more use of pointers by using an array of pointers to store a string array.

The program is illustrated in Fig. 10.9. It's considerably longer and more complicated than any of the C programs that we have looked at so far, and there are several new points embedded within it. One of these is the getline() function, which has been taken from the fount of all C knowledge, the book by Kernighan and Ritchie. The getline() function will get a string named s from the keyboard, and returns a filled string along with an integer equal to string length which need not be used. The important point about the routine is that the string length is limited, and this will ensure that the array declared size is not exceeded. When you make use of strings, it's always important to make sure that a string is not overfilled, because this can create the most remarkable garbage when you try to use such strings.

The first part of the program opens a file called strfil which is intended to take a number of strings, count by the do . . . while loop from 0 to 10, eleven in all. Each string is obtained from the keyboard by using getline(str), the function which assigns the string to the name that is supplied, limits, the string to a maximum of 80 characters, and returns an integer equal to string length. The string is then saved to a disk file by using the usual fprintf routine. Once all of the strings have been read and filed, the file is closed, and the first part of the program ends.

The replay starts with the 'Press RETURN key' type of statement that we encountered earlier, using getchar(). The file pointer is allocated for a read file, and tested in case the file does not exist. Once again, no attempt is made to return to the waiting loop at this stage. The file reading loop makes use of the function fgets. This takes three parameters, str, n,fp, which denote the string, number of characters and file-pointer respectively. The function will read the file whose pointer is fp and return a string of lup to n − 1 characters from the file. Each string is then printed,

```
#include <stdio.h>
main()
{
int n;
FILE *fp;
char str[80],*sp;
n=1;
fp=fopen("strfil","w");
 do
  {printf("Name, please\n");
    getline(str,80);
    fprintf(fp,"%s",str);
   }
 while (++n<=10);
fclose(fp);
printf("\n Press RETURN to continue\n");
getchar();
fp=fopen("strfil","r");
 if (fp==0)
 printf("\n No such file \n");
while (sp=fgets(str,80,fp))
 {
  if (sp==0) break;
  printf("%s",str);
 }
 fclose(fp);
}
getline(s,n)
char s[];
int n;
{
 int c,i;
 i=0;
 while (--n>0 && (c=getchar())!=EOF && c!='\n')
  s[i++]=c;
 if (c=='\n') s[i++]=c;
s[i]='\0';
return(i);
}
```

Figure 10.9 Creating and printing a file of strings, using fgets to read the strings from the file.

and the printing line uses %s to specify a string, but no \n to force a new-line. This is because the strings already have newline characters included when they are put into the file.

All of the files we have looked at have been serial files, and you may wonder what provisions are made for random access files. This depends entirely on your library, because standard C does not prescribe anything other than the basics. You will probably find, however, that your library contains the function fseek which allows you to locate a position, measured in terms of bytes from the start of a file, the end of a file or the previous position in a file. There should be an extended version, lseek as well, and also the ftell function, which returns with the current position in a file. These two functions permit random access handling, but because this is not really a topic for beginners to a language it will be omitted here.

One last point for the moment about files concerns the library functions. A lot of library functions have evolved in a fairly haphazard way, so that there are duplications of purpose. For example, getc(fp) is identical to fgetc(fp), and putc(c,fp) is identical to fputc((c),(fp)), and getchar() is just getc(stdin). This allows the library to be smaller than you might expect, because the duplications can be dealt with by #define lines in the stdio.h header. You do not, however, have to worry about this; simply pick the functions that you want to use and forget about the duplicates.

More structured types

We have come quite a long way in looking at examples and applications of C, but there are still plenty topics to get to grips with. One of these is records, something that is not easy at the best of times, and more difficult if you have only ever programmed in BASIC. A record is a collection of items of data, which may all be of the same type or, more usually, of different types. What makes these items into parts of a record is that they are related.

To take an example, suppose that you wanted to keep a record of membership of the local football club. You would need the name and the address for each member. These would be strings, arrays of type char. You might also want to keep year of birth (because juniors pay a reduced fee, and senior citizen members pay only entry fees), and year of joining (members with ten or twenty years membership have special privilege years). All of these last three items could also be stored as strings or as integers. There might also be an entry for fees due (a float number in a real-life program) and whether paid or not to date.

Now all of this data constitutes a record because for each person, the subject of the record, all the items belong together. It would not make much sense to keep a file of names, one of addresses, one of year of birth, and so on, and yet this is the way that we are often forced to keep such records in BASIC. The alternative in BASIC is often to pack all the data into one string of set length, and to make up a string array.

C allows you to define what will go into a record, and then to create an array of records. Obviously, the ultimate aim of such an array would be to record it on disk, something that is relatively straightforward because C allows you to specify a record as a variable type. The type of variable that is used in C for a record is called a *structure*.

```
struct footballclub {
  char name[20];
  char address[40];
  char birth[5];
  char join [5];
  float fees;
  char paid;
  }F;
main()
/*as usual from now on:*/
```

Figure 10.10 Declaring a structure type. This must be carried out before the start of the main program in which the structure will be used.

We'll start by considering what we need to do in Fig. 10.10 to declare a structure, using as an example the football club illustration above. The first action, as usual, is to declare any constants, so that following any #include lines that were needed we would have #define lines for constants, and then any other definitions that were needed. The important part, however, is what follows in the struct declaration. The name of the record is given as footballclub. This is a reminder only, because though we could use this as a variable name, it's rather unwieldy, as you'll see. The name that is used here is sometimes called the 'tag' of the structure. The structure footballclub is declared, and what follows within curly brackets must be a list of the fields of the record, meaning the items that make up the record.

I have typed these indented, with one item per line, to make them more obvious, and to show the semicolon that follows each declaration. Like any other declaration, the items could be grouped with all the char names following the char heading, separated by commas. The name and address fields are both strings, but with different numbers of characters. The two years are also taken as strings, with the dimensioning for five characters in the year because there will be four digits and the '0' which marks the end of the string. If you don't dimension adequately, the program will compile and run, but the results will be decidedly odd! The fee amount should be a 'float' number – in a program which was seriously intended to keep records of this type, the amount of the subscription would be calculated from a formula, and printed when required, but in this example, I have made it an entered float item.

The latter paid is of type char, and will be used for a 'Y' or 'N' reply, because the subscription will either be paid or not – this club doesn't allow instalment payments! The end of the definition of the fields of this record is marked with the usual } sign. All of this definition occurs before the start of the main program, and following the curly bracket which ends the structure definition, we must have a semicolon. If there is only a semicolon, then the name of the structure can be assigned later by using a line like:

    struct footballclub F;

By using the syntax: }F;, however, we can use F to mean a structure of type footballclub without using another line, which is much more convenient. We could, if we liked, declare other names in this way, such as : }G,H,J; so as to mean that G, H, and K were all names for structures of the type footballclub.

```
/*getting items into fields*/
printf("\n Name please\n");
gets(F.name);
printf("\n Address..\n");
gets(F.address);
printf("\n Year of birth?\n");
gets(F.birth);
/*and so on*/
```

Figure 10.11 How the items of the structure can be referred to at the input stages.

The main program then starts, and the example stops here because what follows depends on what you want to do, and there is no point in having large examples. The important point to note is how the inputs are assigned, as Fig. 10.11 shows. For the name entry, for example, we use gets(F.name). This calls function gets(), and assigns the string that it gets from the keyboard to variable G.name. This is the way that we can select one item (or field) of a record, using the structure variable name, then a full-stop, then the item name. This syntax lets you assign to an item in a structure or print an item. When you want to use scanf for the entry of a float, you will need to use something like &F.fees, and, as you might expect, if you want to do anything more complicated you need, as always, to use pointers. The rest of the information is then entered in the same way, and when you want to print the details on the screen, you use the same syntax of structure name-dot-fieldname. For example, you would use a line such as:

    printf("\n%s",F.name);

to print the name that had been entered into a structure. The structure is from then onwards treated like any other data type, so that you can use arrays of structures, pointers to structures, pointer arrays of structures, files of structures and so on.

The older versions of C did not allow you to transfer data from one structure to another. If you had declared two structures, perhaps F and G of the same type, then you had to transfer their contents by using lines such as:

    strcpy(G.name,F.name)

for each element of the structure. Modern C compilers now allow the much more straightforward:

    G = F

to assign all of one structure to all of another. This is closer to the syntax of PASCAL, and a considerable improvement on the original C. The Zorland compiler supports this updated syntax, as will other modern compilers. You can also pass structure names to functions now, rather than the pointer in the form &G as was previously necessary.

Filing structures

The structure in C is so useful as a way of packing information into groups, particularly in the modern version, that we need some way of recording structures on disk. It would be pleasant if we had a structure filing statement which allowed a complete structure to be put on to disk simply by using the structure name, as we have in PASCAL. This, however, can't be done in standard C because there is no structure filing function, and we have to record the items of a structure one by one. Though this could be done as part of a main program, we'll learn a lot more about the use of structures and pointers if we make the structure filing routine part of a function which we can then use for filing structures of that type.

The important point here is that in older versions of C you can't pass the name of a structure to a function and expect it to do anything about it. You can, however, pass a pointer to a structure by using the & sign with the structure name. This is needed so often that C has a special way of indicating the items in a structure by way of the pointer. For example, if sp is the pointer to a structure, then sp − >item will refer to the field called item in the structure. The − > sign uses the minus and greater-than

```
/*called by recfil(fp,&F) */
/* an imaginary function */
recfil(fp,sp)
struct footballclub *sp;
int *fp;
{
 fprint(fp,"%s\n%s\n",sp->name,sp->address);
 fprint(fp,"%s\n%s\n",sp->birth,sp->join);
 fprint(fp,"%f\n%c\n",sp->fees,sp->paid);
}
```

Figure 10.12 Using a pointer to a structure, and how the items within the structure are referred to by pointer – > name.

signs together. With a modern version of C, simpler methods can be used, but in the following examples, the older pattern will be shown because this is the form you are more likely to see in listings for some time to come.

A sample piece of structure-filing program is illustrated in Fig. 10.12. We assume that a disk file has been opened for writing, using the file pointer fp. The setup of the structure is the same as before, as is the entry of information. After the Y/N information on payment of subscriptions has been entered, a function recfil(fp,&F) is called to place the data of the structure on file. This function uses the file pointer for the disk, fp, an integer, and the other is the structure pointer sp which has been declared as struct footballclub *sp. This declaration is that sp is a pointer to a structure of type footballclub. The other fields of the structure are then sent to the file, using fprintf statements. The name and address strings are sent first, using ''%s%s'' as the specifier for the two strings, and with sp – >name, sp – >address as the separate fields. The other fields of the structure are dealt with in the same way, remembering that sp – >fees is a float, and sp – > paid is a single character. Since the items that are to be recorded are stored in a buffer until the buffer fills or the file is closed, you don't necessarily hear much activity from the disk at the time when this function runs.

Reading back structures

Reading back a file of structures from the disk normally uses fscanf, but you must remember that this function works with pointers. In addition, fscanf will take the end of a string as being the first whitespace in the string, meaning the first blank or any other character which does not 'belong' in a string, such as the TAB key or the space key. This makes fscanf normally more suited for files of integers, or of strings which can be guaranteed to have no spaces in them, but it's not very useful for the type of string that we now want to read, with names and addresses. If you are using the Zorland compiler, you can make use of the extended fscanf which allows you to specify that any string of characters will be accepted, and nominate exceptions which will terminate the string.

If you do not have this extension, then the library contains the useful fgets() function, which is very similar to gets(), but with subtle differences. This function can be used to read back all of the recorded strings, and will not give trouble if any whitespace is found in a string. That doesn't mean that everything is plain sailing, because when you use a library function you have to read the smallprint (or its listing) to see just what it will do with the data.

The similarity between fgets and gets, as defined in Kernighan and Ritchie, is close, but one difference is very important. Whereas gets will read a string of characters, including the RETURN/ENTER character, and then replace the RETURN/ENTER character by a zero to act as string terminator, fgets does not do this. The fgets function reads a string until the '\n' character is found, and then adds a zero to the end of this. This makes the string longer. For example, if year of birth is entered as a string of four characters, it will be recorded as five characters (the '\n' being the fifth), and will be returned into the program as a string of six characters in all, including the '\n' and the '\0'. This means that we have to be careful about dimensioning the strings that we shall read into, because it's easy to fall into the trap of assuming that the string we read back will be the same as we recorded.

The other point to watch is that fgets takes three parameters, the string name, a string length number, and the filepointer. The string length number decides how many of the characters of the string are read and the function reads characters until this number is exceeded or until a newline character is found. Unless you are very sure of your string lengths, it's better to provide generous values of length, so that the newline character ends the reading action. If, of course, all of the string were tested for length before recording, there's no objection to counting them back precisely. What you need to remember, however, is that the number that you provide for string length in fgets must be the complete string length, including the ending zero and newline character.

With these warnings in mind, we can now look at what is needed to read back the string file that was created by a program that used a section such as that illustrated in Fig. 10.12. It's likely that we would want to read the structures back into an array, and this will mean that an array of structures must be declared. The important point then is how each structure field in each item of the array should be referred to. A section of a suitable reading program is shown in Fig. 10.13.

```
/* all placed within a FOR loop*/
fgets(F[j].name,20,fp);
fgets(F[j].address,40,fp);
fgets(F[j].birth,6,fp);
fgets(F[j].join,6,fp);
/* and so on */
/* can then use */
printf("%s\n",F[j].name);
/* and so on */
```

Figure 10.13   Entering items into an array of structures.

Earlier in the program, the structure will have been named as F[2000] (or whatever dimensioning is needed), and a separate count number could be included in another file as a way of ensuring that the reading and writing programs do not get out of step. In BASIC, this number would be read and used to dimension the array. In C this sort of thing is not so easy because a structure array has to be dimensioned before the main program starts. If the structure declaration is made before the start of the main program (that is, all of struct footballclub but without the F[2000], then the declaration of the name (F) and the dimensioning could be done in a function, with the structure not used in the main program. This function would have to be called after the count number was loaded from disk.

Working with structure files

The part-example of Fig. 10.13 showed the construction of a reading part of a file that would create an array of structures. A normal action from then on would be to pick out one record, or to sort the records into alphabetical order. Now picking out one record is fairly simple, as the program section of Fig. 10.14 shows. The records are assumed to have been read as an array of structures, using fgets(), which will result in each string ending with a '\n' and a zero.

The test for equality of strings is used to make the loop run faster by using a continue in the for loop if the strings are not equal. When a matching string is found, the else section runs, printing the details for the selected name. Before the loop started, integer x was made equal to 'false' (zero), and if a string match is found, this integer x becomes true, and the loop breaks. In this way, the loop runs fast until a matching string is found, and then breaks immediately afterwards. The integer x is used after the loop ends to print a suitable message if no matching name has been found.

```
/* count is number of records */
/* read into array F[] */
printf("\n Please type name required \n");
gets(s);
x=false;
/* defined as 0, true as 1 */
for (j=0;j<=count-1;j++)
 {
 if (strcmp(s,F[j].name)) continue;
 else;
  {
  printf("%s\n",F[j].name);
  /* and so on............*/
  x=true;
  }
 break;
 }
if (x==false)printf("\n Name not found.");
/* continue main */
```

Figure 10.14 A fragment of program that illustrates how one record can be picked out from an array.

Sorting a file

In BASIC, there is nothing that corresponds to the structure. This makes actions such as sorting very tedious in most varieties of BASIC, because each field of a record has to be represented by an array item or as part of a string. Sorting is never easy, but in C you do at least have the advantage of a sort routine called qsort in the library. The illustration of Fig. 10.15 shows a Shell-Metzner type of sort routine used to sort a list of records in alphabetical order of names as typed in the file. Now this is not the type of sort which is included in the library, because that one is a rather complicated general-purpose one, nor is it the sort that is mentioned in Kernighan and Ritchie's book. For the sake of variety and also to show how such functions are written, I have put in another Shell type of sort, adapted from a version which I wrote in PASCAL.

As before, we assume that the program has read the structures into an array. Because it's more convenient for the sort routine, the array numbers start with 1 rather than with 0, but that's the only change up to the point where we take up the listing. In the structure declaration, the usual F[2000] dimensioning will have been supplemented by *Fp, making Fp a pointer to a structure. Simply declaring that Fp is a pointer,

```
/* read in with fgets into  */
/* array F[j] as usual */
/* declarations not shown */
Fp=F;
y=1;
while (y<count)
 y=2*y;
do
 {
  y=(y-1)/2;
  it=count-y;
  for (i=1;i<=it;i++)
   {
    j=i;
    do
     {
     z=j+y;
     if (strcmp (F[z].name,F[j].name)<=0)
      {
      swap (Fp+z,Fp+j,sizeof(struct footballclub));
      j=j-y;
      }
     else j=0;
     }
    while (j>0);
   }
 }
while (y!=1);
/* can now print sorted list */
```

Figure 10.15 Another fragment of program, this time showing a Shell-Metzner sort routine in use. For string sorts, always convert to upper-case for sorting and back afterwards.

however, doesn't make it point to anything, and the statement *Fp = F is needed to make Fp a pointer to the start of structure F. This is a very important step, and omitting it is one of the most common errors in the use of pointers. If your pointer hasn't been set to point at something, then trouble, in the shape of a major program crash, can't be far behind. Why do we need the pointer anyhow? The answer is that in the sort routine, we shall want to change the pointers to different members of the array. Changing pointers involves exchanging only two numbers, rather than the set of strings (or whatever else is used) in a structure. For this reason, it's fast and simple.

I won't go into details of how the Shell-Metzner sort works, because it's a standard routine that you can find described at length in many other books. The important features of the sort (starting at the statement y = y + 1) are the test and exchange steps. The test uses strcmp as you would expect, with F[].name being used as a basis of comparison. The exchange step uses a function swap, and the parameters that are supplied make use of the string pointers, along with the sizeof statement. The sizeof function, as its name suggests, will provide an integer, the number of bytes of memory allocated to a variable. The swap routine exchanges pointers, if need be, and when the sort is completed, the structures will be in order of names. If the swap routine is not in your library, then you can use the version that was illustrated earlier in Fig. 7.9.

The important point is that, because of the *Fp = F step, you can print out this new order using F[j], you don't have to use pointer Fp unless you want to. This is the value of altering pointers in this way, because the pointers can be altered in a subroutine and the alteration will affect the result of a printout in the main routine. In this example, the whole sort routine is, unusually, in the main program, simply to avoid

```
/* nested structure example */
struct name{
   char sur[20];
   char frn[20];
   };
struct dob{
   int day;
   int month;
   int year;
   };
struct person{
   struct name memname;
   struct dob birth;
   char phone[16];
   }member[max];
main()
/* main starts here */
/* to refer to an item, we use */
/* lines such as the following  */
/* printf("\n%s",member[j].memnam.sur); */
/* gets surname of member   */
/* printf("\n%s",member[j].memnam,frn); */
/* gets forename of same member */
/* and so on */
```

Figure 10.16 An example of the formation and use of nested structures.

the problems of passing parameters until you have seen an example of the straightforward version.

Record nests and choices

So far, each record that we have illustrated has consisted of items that are simple variables. We can, however, use records which consist partly or completely of other records! Structures which are a part of another structure are called 'nested' structures, and typically they are used to hold details of an entry. We might, for example, have an entry called birth which would require the details of day, month and year of birth. This could be provided by making birth a structure in itself, with day, month and year items of that structure. Figure 10.16 shows how this provision for nested structures can be used.

The main structure now is of type person, but it now contains the substructures name and dob. The structure variable memnam is of type name, and birth is of type dob, both of which must be defined as structures before the main structure can be defined. Structure name is defined as consisting of sur and frn, both arrays of char. Remember that you can't use for for forename, because this is a reserved word. The structure dob consists of day, month and year, all integers. These ranges would, in a working program, be checked each time an item was entered.

The important feature now is that a reading or printing line uses the full title for each field and subfield. For the first member whose surname we want, we have to specify:

    member[j].memnam.sur

using the main structure title, the substructure title (memnam) and the field title of sur. Each entry, replay and print action will use these specifiers in this way.

The union

A union is a 'hold anything' variable that is really just another form of a structure which can be used to hold a character, integer, float, string or whatever you like. It sound splendid but in fact it's not used as much as you might expect. A union has to be declared in very much the same way as a structure is declared, using a pattern of the form shown in Fig. 10.17. In this example, the type union is declared with the pattern name of boss. The union can contain a character, a pointer or an integer called j.

Note that this is one *or* another. A structure, by contrast contains all of the types that are specified in its declaration, the union contains any one. In the lines that follow the declaration, a type is assigned and its value then printed out. The important point is that you can assign only one value at a time and you must select the correct name such as chief.c,

```
/* nested structure example */
struct name{
  char sur[20];
  char frn[20];
  };
struct dob{
  int day;
  int month;
  int year;
  };
struct person{
  struct name memname;
  struct dob birth;
  char phone[16];
  }member[max];
main()
/* main starts here */
/* to refer to an item, we use */
/* lines such as the following  */
/* printf("\n%s",member[j].memnam.sur); */
/* gets surname of member  */
/* printf("\n%s",member[j].memnam,frn); */
/* gets forename of same member */
/* and so on */
```

Figure 10.17 The declaration of type union and a simple example of its use.

chief.j or whatever is needed. You can declare an array of unions, and store different items in different elements.

When a union variable is declared, it will reserve as much memory space as is needed for the largest of its possible contents. If you make a union type, for example, which contains a character, an integer and a four-character string, then the string is the longest member and will make the union five bytes long (don't forget the final 0). A structure similarly declared would need one byte for the character, two for the integer and five for the string, making a total of eight bytes.

If you attempt to print out data that has not been assigned to the union, you will get garbage. For example, if you have assigned a string to your union as chief.s, then trying to printout a character chief.c may produce the first character of the string (this depends on your compiler), but attempting to print an integer chief.j will certainly result in garbage.

11
Miscellany

Though we have come a considerable way from Chapter 1, we have only introduced the elements of the C language. Many aspects of C require you to have more than a passing acquaintance with how the PC works, and until you are familiar with items like interrupts and stack sizes, then the use of these library functions are very definitely not for you. This chapter is devoted to some actions and features of C which have not conveniently fitted into the previous chapters, and is more specific to the Zorland compiler in the sense that some Zorland library functions will be mentioned which will not necessarily be available if you are using a different compiler. Note that if you use one of the public domain C compilers, the library may be rather limited, but you can often obtain extra library functions in source code from bulletin boards and other sources of public domain software.

Memory allocation

Before we start on some of the groups of library functions, the topic of memory allocation needs some explanation. A BASIC interpreter uses a very simple memory system, with all the variables stored in the space beyond the program code (i.e. at higher memory addresses). The way that memory is allocated by a C compiler depends on how large a program you are creating, because in the PC type of machine the capability to work with large amounts of data is bought at the price of longer access time. For the examples in this book, you will be working with the small memory model, in which your program code occupies one 64K section (or *segment*) of memory, and your data occupies another. If you use EXE2BIN to convert to a .COM file, both program code and data will be placed in the same 64K part of memory.

In the data segment, the memory is used to hold statics, stack and heap data. The lowest memory addresses of this segment are used for static data, holding values of variables that have been defined as static or which have been declared outside main() so that they are global. The next higher range of addresses will be used for the stack, the memory which is changing in content while the program is running. The stack, whose default size is 2048 bytes, is used to contain temporary data such as auto variables and all values that have to be held while a function runs, such as the program code address at which the program resumes after a function is completed. Large memory compilers make use of a separate 64K segment of memory for this stack. Stack memory is used from the top down, in the sense that the first item placed on the stack occupies the highest available address number, the next item goes in the next lower address, and so on. As items are read back, the addresses become available for different data, so that the stack is a very temporary type of memory allocation.

The heap, a concept which is foreign to BASIC programmers, contains memory that has been allocated by the calloc function, something we haven't looked at yet. This region of memory is at a range of addresses higher than the top limit of the stack, and is used from the bottom up, lowest address first, to avoid conflicts with the stack. The form of the calloc function is:

    calloc(50,sizeof(double));

and in this example, the action is to reserve space in the heap for 50 double-precision numbers. To make use of calloc, it has to be declared in the form:

    char *calloc();

and this implies that the number that calloc() returns is a pointer to char. If, as is usual, you want this pointer to be used as a pointer to some other variable, you will have to cast it, using something like:

    dp = (double*) calloc(50, sizeof(double));

with dp then used as a pointer to the start of the piece of memory that will contain 50 double-precision numbers.

The use of calloc is confined to allocation of memory when no other method can be used, mainly when linked lists (not covered in this book) are being created. A linked list consists of a set of structures in which each structure contains a pointer which can be used to hold the address of another structure. It can also be used to ensure that a pointer is correctly assigned to some vacant space, though for this purpose a simpler function malloc is used. The malloc function requires only a single number between the brackets, the number of bytes of memory to allocate. For example, if you had declared a pointer as char *nampoint, then:

    nampoint = (char *)malloc(50);

would allocate 50 bytes of memory from the heap, and assign nampoint with the starting address of this piece of safe memory. This is very similar to the action of declaring nampoint[50]. The use of calloc or malloc in this way ensures that a pointer points to a correctly allocated piece of memory rather than to some randomly assigned part of the system. Heap memory that has been assigned by calloc or malloc in this way can be released by free, and in this sense is more permanent than the stack memory. In a COM type of program, program code, statics, stack and heap are all contained in one single 64K segment.

Command line variables

You very often want to make use of command line variables when you write C programs. You might, for example, write a program that counts the words in a word processor file (yes, they still design word processors with no word count!), and start your program with:

    countem myfile.txt

in which the program is countem.exe and the file is myfile.txt. In this example, myfile.txt is a command line variable, a string that has to be passed to the program to be used as a file name. You could, of course, imagine programs which required a number, a character, or a whole set of variables (separated by spaces) to be passed into a program. How do we do it?

As it happens, the scheme is straightforward once you know the rules. Two variables have to be used, and by convention, they are called argc and argv. These are passed to main, so that the start of your program is written as

```
main(argc,argv)
    char *argv[];
    int argc;
{
rest of the program ...
```

Note that this is the exception to the rule that no parameters are placed inside the brackets of main() and no variables declared between main() and the first curly bracket. Of these variables, argc is a counter, an integer number, and argv is a pointer array, pointing to character strings.

The value of argc will be one more than the number of argument variables following the program name, because the program name itself is counted as an argument for this purpose. Using the command line of countem myfile.txt would therefore give a value for argc of 2. The pointers are then argv[0], which points to 'countem' and argv[1], which points to myfile.txt. Figure 11.1 shows a simple example, in which the name that you type following the program name is printed on the screen, nothing more. Save this under the name argtest and try it.

```
main(argc,argv)
int argc;
char *argv[];
{
 char name[15];
 strcpy(name,argv[1]);
 printf("\n Name is %s",name);
}
```

Figure 11.1 Using a command line variable. This type of programming allows you to pick up as many variables you like from the program command line.

Using your library

The usefulness of C is measured by the extent of your library, and most compilers come with very extensive libraries, enough to permit a much greater range of programming that you are ready for when you first start using C. You should have, either from the compiler manual or from the library disk, a list of the library functions. A list alone is not enough, though, because you need to know at least what each function requires to be passed to it, and what is passed back. This information that should be included in your manual. In some cases, when you are dubious about the action of a function, you need to be able to read the source code, and this is not usually available. Some manufacturers make the whole library available in source code for an additional fee.

The form in which a library function will be shown in your manual will be something like:

```
#include < stdio.h >
char *fgets(str,n,fp)
char *str;
int n;
FILE *fp;
```

This means, reading from the top down, that in order to use this function, the header stdio.h should be read by placing the #include command at the start of the listing. What follows shows the form of the command, fgets in this example, so that you know that three arguments will be needed, and that the function must return a pointer to type char. Of the arguments, str is a string name (string pointer), n is an integer, and fp is a pointer to a file.

If this is all you know of the function, you can use the function, but only in a rather limited way unless you have enough experience of C to guess what is returned. The description in the manual should therefore tell you what is returned, and what the limitations on use will be. You need to know, for example that characters will be read from the file pointed to by fp and placed in the string str until a newline character or an EOF character is read or a read error occurs. You also need to know that the newline is included into the string, which therefore ends with a newline as well as the '\0' character. When the function returns, str will be a string name if all is well, and this pointer will be returned. If there is no file, or an empty file, then the function returns NULL, and str remains as it was before using the function. If a read error is encountered part-way through the read, NULL is returned, but str contains the characters that were read before the error occurred.

This detailed information will generally be available to you for all the functions that are supplied with your compiler, but it may be that you have bought additional libraries. If so, you will have to make sure that you have or can get this type of full information, without which you are using the library in the dark. In some cases, if a library is supplied in source code, no explanations may be available on the basis that you can read all the detail from the source code. That's fine once you have some experience, but it's never easy to read someone else's code, and a full explanation is always preferable.

Library groups

In any library for the PC, there will be some large groups of library routines all of which serve a similar area of need. Examples include the input/output functions, character handlers, string functions, screen handling, sound, mouse control, time/date use and so on. In this section we'll look at some of the function names that are available with the standard Zorland library, because many of these functions will probably be useful to you and many are likely to be included (some with different names) in other libraries.

The input/output functions of the Zorland library are of two main groups. The low-level routines work directly with the MS-DOS system, and work with 'raw' files in the sense that each character in the file is used with no amendments; as a binary file. Unless you particularly need such routines, and know what you (and they) are doing, you should avoid them. The low level functions are creat(), open(), close(), 1seek(), read() and write().

The more important functions are the 'high-level' types which make use of the low-level functions in a pre-determined way. Each one requires the use of a pointer to type FILE when used for disk input/output, but for other inputs and outputs, the names that start with std are used. These names are shown in Fig. 11.2(a), and will be supplied for you by using the stdio.h header at the start of a program. In this way, you do not

Name	Action
stdin	keyboard
stdout	screen
stderr	error report to screen
stdaux	AUX: output
stdprn	printer

(a)

```
#include <stdio.h>
main()
{
char c;
while((c=getc(stdin))!='\n')
putc(c,stdout);
}
```

(b)

Figure 11.2 (a) The standard names for inputs and outputs. (b) Using the standard names in input/output routines.

need to specify in a printf instruction that the destination of the data is the screen, but you can, if you want, specify these names as file pointers in the getc and putc functions, as Fig. 11.2(b) shows. Figure 11.3 shows the complete list of input/output functions for Zorland C.

The character package is often referred to as the 'is' package, because each function name starts with is. Using these functions requires the ctype.h header, and each takes an argument which is a character variable. The quantity returned will be either true or false depending on the character that is being tested. Figure 11.4 is a list of the functions and their actions, some of which have been illustrated in the preceding chapters.

The str package consists of the functions which manipulate strings. The list of functions in this group varies from one compiler to another, unlike the is set, and Fig. 11.5 shows the 19 strong Zorland set, with notes. A good set of string functions allows you even better string handling that a good BASIC, and will include some functions that you might have some difficulty in finding a use for.

When we get to screen handling, functions become more specialised, and what is provided can vary considerably from one compiler to another. Zorland offers a 'display package' of simple screen handling functions, and will provide as an extra a full set of window routines. The Zorland display package requires close compatibility with the IBM PC, because the screen actions are obtained by writing bytes directly into the screen memory. This ensures fast action, but is possible only on a

---

Low level:

creat()	create a new file, overwriting any of same name.
open()	open a file.
close()	close a file.
lseek()	find position in file.
read()	read binary file.
write()	write binary file.

These low level functions work with a 'file handle' number, of which the following are reserved:

0	keyboard
1	screen
2	error output to screen
3	AUX: output
4	printer.

Low level functions should not be mixed with high level functions on the same file.

High level:

All of these functions are buffered and act through a file pointer fp (which is declared as FILE*) to the file stream.

fclose(fp)	flush buffers, close file.
feof(fp)	0 if not at last record in file.
ferror(fp)	check error flag on file stream.
fflush(fp)	flush buffer on file stream.
fgetc(fp)	get next character from file stream.
fgets(s,n,fp)	reads string from fp to name s. Ends after n − 1 characters or at newline, end of file, or read error.
fileno (fp)	returns file number of fp.
fp = fopen(n,m)	returns fp of file name n, mode m.
fputc(c,fp)	writes char c to file fp.
fputs(s,fp)	writes string s to fp.
fread(p,x,n,fp)	reads n items of x bytes each into array p.
freopen(n,m,fp)	closes file name n, mode m.

continued

fscanf(fp,args)	as for scanf, streams fp.
fseek(fp,s,o)	sets file position in fp at s bytes from o.
ftell(fp)	returns current position in fp.
fwrite(p,x,n,fp)	write n items length x bytes from array p.
getc(fp)	get next character from fp.
fprintf(fp,args)	as printf, but to file fp.
putc(fp)	put character to file fp.
ungetc(c,fp)	put character c back on file fp.

Figure 11.3 The input and output functions of Zorland C.

All of these functions operate on a character c, and the action is detected by returning non-zero (TRUE).

Main	Action
isalnum(c)	letter or digit
isalpha(c)	letter
isascii(c)	code less than 128
iscntrl(c)	less than 32 or equal to 127
isdigit(c)	digit 0 to 9
isgraph(c)	printing character other than space
islower(c)	lower-case character
isprint(c)	printing character
ispunct(c)	punctuation character
isspace(c)	whitespace character
isupper(c)	upper-case
isxdigit(c)	character 0 to 9, A to F or a to f (hex digits)

Associated with this set is the TO set of:

toascii(c)	zero bit 7 (remainder range 0 to 127)
tolower(c)	convert to lower-case
toupper(c)	convert to upper-case

Figure 11.4 The Zorland is package, allowing operations on single characters.

Most of these functions return a pointer to type char, and operate on strings s1, s2. A few return an integer, and some require an integer n to specify a number for string length.

strcat(s1,s1)	add s2 to end of s1, return s1 pointer.
strcmp(s1,s2)	compare s1 and s2, zero if identical.
strcmpl(s1,s2)	as strcmp, but ignores case of letters.
strcpy(s1,s2)	copies s2 to s1, return s1 pointer.
strcspn(s1,s2)	points to last part of s1 that contains s2.
strdup(s1)	points to copy of s1 allocated by malloc call.
strlen(s1)	number of characters in s1, excluding \0.
strlwr(s1)	converts s1 to lower-case.
strncat(s1,s2,n)	adds maximum of n characters from s2 to s1.
strncmp(s1,s2,n)	compares n characters of strings only.
strncpy(s1,s2,n)	copies maximum of n characters from s2 to s1.
strpbrk(s1,s2)	points to first character in s1 that is also in s2.
strrchr(s1,c)	points to last occurrence of c in s1.
strrev(s1)	reverses order of characters in s1.
strset(s1,c)	makes string s1 consist of characters c.
strspn(s1,s2)	gives length of first portion in s1 made out of s2.
strtok(s1,s2)	points to string s1 with terminator s2.
strupr(s1)	converts s1 to upper-case.
swab(s1,s2,n)	copies n bytes from s1 to s2, swapping pairs of bytes.

Figure 11.5 The Zorland string function package, which gives an excellent selection of very useful string handling actions. One point to watch is that strncpy creates a string with no terminating zero if the copied string is shorter than the original string.

machine that uses exactly the same addresses for the screen positions as the IBM machine. Figure 11.6 lists these functions, with brief notes. If you want to write such items for yourself on a less-compatible machine, one method is to run the program (ANSI.COM) that makes the screen obey the ANSI standard codes, and then write functions that contain printf or preferably puts lines that contain the required codes (notes in your computer manual).

The Zorland sound package contains sound_tone, which will play a note whose number of cycles and cycle time are specified as arguments. The sound_beep function makes a note of constant duration, using a

All of the screen package functions return void, and most require no arguments. Any program that uses them should be preceded by #include < disp.h >.

Function	Action
disp__close	flush output, end use of display functions.
disp-eeol	delete from cursor to end of line.
disp-eeop	delete from cursor to end of screen page.
disp__endstand	end reverse video mode.
disp__flush	flush output to update display.
disp__move(r,c)	move cursor to row r, column c.
disp__open	initialise display functions.
disp__pokew(r,c,a)	place attribute/character combination (as integer) into row r, column c.
disp__printf(f,a)	write to screen directly, using printf format.
disp__putc(c)	write character c to specified screen location.
disp__setarr(n)	modifies attribute of character (see disp.h file).
disp__startstand	display following characters in inverse video.

Figure 11.6 The Zorland display package, the set of functions that allows screen handling on a close-compatible machine such as the Amstrad models. For more advanced uses, there are add-on graphics and window-handling libraries.

frequency determined by the argument number. The sound__click function causes only a click, and its main use is to provide a keyclick sound. These actions are illustrated in Fig. 11.7

For more specialised uses, there is also the Mouse package, offering complete control of a mouse that is of the Microsoft type. This package

void sound__tone(x,y,z)	sound note of tone number x, with y% high and z low output. Values of x and y are usually 50 each.
void sound__beep(x)	sound brief beep; x = 1331 gives 1 kHz.
void sound__click()	make click sound.

Other sound outputs are obtained by writing suitable numbers direct to the ports.

Figure 11.7 The Zorland sound package.

requires good knowledge of mouse programming methods, and is definitely not for the beginner. The time package allows date and time to be handled, and is also not for the beginner. Note that on the Amstrad it is usually necessary to run the RTC program in order to make the clock of the Amstrad machine available to programs running in the machine.

Pointers to functions

By the time you have reached this place in this book, your 'L' plates will be ready to remove, and we'll end with a fragment of more advanced C use. I must emphasise that this is just a fragment, and the next step in a serious study of C has to be programming for yourself, preferable with a copy of Kernighan and Ritchie close by. In these closing pages, however, we can look at another useful topic, pointers to functions.

Everything in C has a pointer, and a function is no exception, since the code of a function will be stored in the memory starting at some address, and the address number can be stored as a pointer variable. The two things that C allows you to do with a function are to call it and to find its pointer, and we have had adequate experience of the first of these. When you first start to learn to program in C, pointer to functions are not a pressing necessity, but there can come a time when the use of a function pointer is the easiest way out of a problem. The action, basically, is of allowing you to select which of a number of functions you want to select.

A very simple example of the use of a pointer to a function is illustrated in Fig. 11.8. The example is such an elementary one that it could be done much more easily by other methods, but as always, simple examples are easier to learn from. In this example, the program is provided with a word that is typed partly in upper-case and partly in lower-case, and the aim is to reverse the case of each letter by calling appropriate functions.

The main program is simple enough, but the declarations have to be watched. The functions that are going to be passed as parameters have to be declared at the start of this main program, and are called down and up, and each of them will return an integer. Following the declarations, the program starts a loop in which each character of the word is selected and passed as a parameter to a function called redo. This function does not need to be declared in the main program, and will be designed so as to return the character rather then altering a pointer. Because it returns a character, its form is:

    character = function(parameters);

and in the example, the two different calls to redo are placed in two test lines. If the character that is being dealt with has an ASCII code of less

```
main()
{
static char test[]="tEsT";
int down(),up();
/*these are functions returning int */
int j;
printf("\n%s",test);
for (j=0;j<=3;j++)
{
if (test[j]<91) test[j]=redo (test[j],up);
else if (test[j]>96) test[j]=redo(test[j],down);
}
printf("\n%s",test);
}
redo(c,change)
char c;
int (*change)();
{
c=(*change)(c);
return(c);
}
up(s)
char s;
{
s+=32;
return(s);
}
down(s)
char s;
{
s-=32;
return(s);
}
```

Figure 11.8 Passing pointers to functions. This allows a routine to select which function will be used, as this simple program demonstrates.

than 91, then it is an upper-case character and function up must be called within the redo function. This is done by using the call:

test[j] = redo(test[j],up);

in which we want to alter test[j] by equating it to the character returned by redo. We also want redo to make use of function up and this function name is put into the parameter list for redo. Note that we use up and not &up because C takes the name of a function, like the name of an array, as a read-only pointer to where that function starts. The alternative call is made if test[j] gives an ASCII code greater than 91, when the call to redo makes use of the function down.

The next step is to look at function redo to see how the alternative functions up, down are used. The header for redo uses parameters c,change in which c is a character and change represents the pointer to a function passed by redo. This function represented by change has to be declared before opening the curly bracket on redo, and it is declared as:

```
int (*change)();
```

a function that returns an integer and whose temporary name is pointed to by change. You must use the name as a pointer here, with the asterisk, and the brackets surrounding the function name, plus a separate set of brackets for parameters as you would have with any function. The redo action then consists only of calling the function that has been passed to redo and returning the correct character. Once again, however, the correct syntax is important. The temporary name must be used as a pointer and enclosed in brackets, with its parameter c in separate brackets following (*change). Since this function needs to return a character, we use:

```
c = (*change)(c);
return(c);
```

to ensure the return of a suitably changed character. The effect of all this will be to pass the pointer to one of the functions up or down and execute the action of that function from within redo. The functions up,down are written conventionally.

Passing function names in this way is particularly useful when you want to use a function on different types of data. One very common type of action is sorting lists of different items. This can call for the use of different comparison functions, one for numbers, one for strings, and different exchange functions, but with the same basic action, such as the quicksort. This type of use is illustrated in Kernighan and Ritchie.

ANSI committee changes

Most of the books on C were written up to ten years before the ANSI committee recommended some changes, mainly to the way in which C can be written, and aiming at making a C listing clearer to read and allowing compilers to pick up errors in a more satisfactory way. All modern compilers for the PC ought to incorporate these improvements, which are outlined here.

The first improvement relates to the description of a function which normally would be declared in the form int funct, and described in the form:

```
int funct(a,b)
int *a,*b;
```

in a manual. The recommended method now is to use what is termed a *function prototype*, meaning that the declaration of the function carries much more information, in the style:

```
int funct(int *a, int *b)
```

and using an identical line is the description. This allows the compiler to check the parameters to a function and report an error if they are of the wrong type. It can also cause a cast action to be performed automatically by specifying a type – an example of this is illustrated in the Zorland manual.

Another extension which is very useful allows the use of an enumerated data type as in PASCAL. An enumerated data type allows you to work with numbers that represent items in a data list. You might, for example, represent the months of the year by number 0 to 11, using lines likes:

```
#define January 0
#define February 1
#define March 2
```

and so on. Modern compilers will allow you to replace this by a line such as:

```
enum year { January, February, March ... };
```

following which you can use a declaration such as enum year Y so as to be able to assign Y = April, after which the value of Y would be 3, the number associated with April in the list. Enumerated types are stored as integers, and can be cast as integers. For more details of the use of enumerated types you will need a handbook of PASCAL, since few books on C have caught up with this change.

A very welcome improvement is that one structure can now be assigned to another, as has been illustrated, and one union to another, with a considerable reduction in the source code. Structures can also now be passed to functions and returned from functions using the structure name rather than a separate pointer. The compiler will now pick up any attempt to make a reference to an incorrect structure member formed by using one structure name with the field of another structure. In other words, if you have structures A, with fields F1, F2, F3 and Z with fields G1, G2, G3, you cannot use a reference such as A.G2 now. In the past, this type of error was not picked up.

The specifier void, which has been used in the past, is now officially part of the language, and is used to show that a function returns nothing. Previously, many compilers declared void to mean integer. It is also possible now to write a string in several lines, using double quotes on each line. A hex number can be written as, for example, \x2F (rather than 0x2F), and type char is taken as unsigned rather than signed (though you can specify a signed char if you should happen to want it).

Finally, there are minor changes to typedef. This is a part of C that has not been covered in this book, because it's not an action that anyone beginning C is likely to want to use. The action of typedef is to allow a name to be used for an existing type, so that:

    typedef int width;

will make the word 'width' be in every way equivalent to int so that you can declare variables of type width. The Kernighan and Ritchie book describes typedef, so that the principle is not new, and the changes affect only the checking that the compiler carries out on variables that have been declared in this way.

Endgame

From now on, you can consider yourself cast on the open C, but not, I hope, adrift. The way forward is very much guided by your own inclinations, because you should know what type of programs you want to write, and that requirement will decide which aspects of C you need most experience with. As with any major programming language, you cannot expect to have mastery of all of C unless you happen to be writing C compilers. If, for example, you specialise in short utilities, the language requirements will amount to little more than disk input/output and character changing. On the other hand, if your interest is in writing major pieces of software such as word processors, spreadsheets, even BASIC (or C) interpreters, then your knowledge and experience of the language has to be extensive, and there is no substitute for varied experience.

Whatever your interest, keeping in touch with the language is always important, so that you should take every opportunity to look at C listings produced by other programmes. The most common phrase that springs to the lips when you do this kind of thing is 'I didn't realise you could do *that*', because a brief description of a process, such as you would find in Kernighan and Ritchie, does not always prompt you to a full understanding of what can be achieved. If you are using the Zorland compiler, then you will probably subscribe to ZC News, the magazine for Zorland users, which contains excellent updating information, programs, items on quirks of the language and all kinds of hints for the programmer at any level. Don't feel left out of it because some of the text looks as if it's aimed at professorial level. Given a few months of specialisation, and that sort of article becomes clear, and if you don't want to specialise in that direction, then there's no point in worrying about it. Happy sailing.

A
One's Complement

The one's complement of a binary number is the result of inverting each digit in the number. Inversion means that each 1 is replaced by a 0 and each 0 by a 1.

For example, the single character number denary 59 is in binary:

    0011   1011

and this complements to:

    1100   0100

which in denary is 196.

For integers using two bytes, the action is identical. The number 1706 in denary is, in binary:

    0000   0110   1010   1010

which complements to:

    1111   1001   0101   0101

giving unsigned denary 63829.

Note that if signed number are used, these results may be shown in negative form. For an integer of two bytes, any number greater than 32767 and less than 65536 will appear as a negative number, the result of subtraction from 65536. The number 63829, for example, will appear as −1707.

B
Other Binary Number Operators

NOTE: These operators are not applied to floats.

The shift operators

The shift operators are $>>$ and $<<$, of which can be used along with two numbers, the number that is to be shifted and the number of places to be shifted. If the shift number is not stated, the default is unity. The syntax is of the form: $x>>y$ where x is the number operated on and y is the number of places to be shifted. The action is most easily illustrated with a single byte char number.

For example, the expression $45<<2$ means a two place left shift of the number 45 in binary. This is:

    0010   1101

and the shifting causes bits to be lost from the left-hand side and zeros to be inserted at the right-hand side. The first shift gives:

    0101   1010 (denary 90)

and the second shift gives:

    1011   0100 (denary 180)

The left shift action has the effect of multiplying numbers by 2, but this will not always appear to be true if the most significant bit (left-hand side) of an integer is changes, because this bit is used as a sign indicator. Even if you work with unsigned numbers, incorrect answers can be obtained because of overflow. For example, the denary integer number 18137 is:

    0100   0110   1101   1001

and shifted three places left gives:

    0011   0110   1100   1000   (denary 14024)

because of the overflow from the left-hand side.

Similarly a right shift is equivalent to an integer division by two, but the displayed result can seem incorrect if there is a change in the most significant bit or if the shifting leaves the number as zero. For example, the short integer -24 is in binary:

1111   1111   1110   1000

and the three-place right shift (division by 8) gives.

0001   1111   1111   1101

which is denary 8189. The problem does not appear if integer numbers are displayed in unsigned form, when the two numbers are shown as 65512 and 8189 respectively.

C
Binary Code

Position values:

Bit.No.	7	6	5	4	3	2	1	0
Value	128	64	32	16	8	4	2	1

For each further place to the left, use a position number which is double the previous one.

Binary count from 0 to 15 denary.

Denary	Binary	Denary	Binary
0	0000	8	1000
1	0001	9	1001
2	0010	10	1010
3	0011	11	1011
4	0100	12	1100
5	0101	13	1101
6	0110	14	1110
7	0111	15	1111

Conversions:

1. Denary to binary. Divide the number by 2, and put the remainder next to it. Do the same with the result of the division, and so on until the last number is zero. Then read the remainders *from the bottom up.*

Example: Conversion of 58 denary.

Number 58 divide by 2 = 29 and 0 over.
          29 divide by 2 = 14 and 1 over.
          14 divide by 2 = 7 and 0 over.
           7 divide by 2 = 3 and 1 over.
           3 divide by 2 = 1 and 1 over.
           1 divide by 2 = 0 and 1 over.

Reading from bottom of remainders gives 111010, which is the binary equivalent. This can be padded out with zeros on the left-hand side to make it an 8-bit or a sixteen-bit number. For example, as an 8-bit number, it would be 00111010.

2. Binary to denary. Write the binary number with the position values above the '1' digits, then add the position values. For example, the binary number 01011011 is written as:

```
    64      16  8      2  1
  0   1   0   1  1  0  1  1
```

The position values added give $64 + 16 + 8 + 2 + 1 = 91$.

Octal numbers
Octal numbers are in a scale of eight. The octal count from 0 to 7 is as in denary, then:

Denary	Octal
8	10
9	11
10	1
..	..
16	20

    etc.

Conversion of denary to octal:

As for denary to binary, but dividing by eight. For example, denary 467 is converted as follows:

$$467 \text{ divide by } 8 = 58 \text{ and } 3 \text{ over.}$$
$$58 \text{ divide by } 8 = 7 \quad \text{ and } 2 \text{ over.}$$
$$7 \text{ divide by } 8 = 0 \quad \text{ and } 7 \text{ over.}$$

This makes the octal number equal to 723.

Octal to denary. As for binary, but use the place numbers:

```
  32768    4096    512    64    8    1
```

For example, the octal number 421 is $4*64 + 2*8 + 1 = 273$ denary.

Octal and Binary

Each octal number corresponds to three bits of binary, from 000 to 111. See the binary number table for these equivalents. To convert octal to binary, simply write down the three-bit binary equivalent of each octal digit. For example, octal 254 becomes:

```
2    5    4
010  101  100
```

giving the binary number 010101100.

For converting from binary to octal, divide the binary number into three-bit groups, starting from the right-hand side. Convert each group into octal, including any one or two bit number at the left-hand side.

For example, the binary number:

1001110110100110 is grouped as:

```
1    001    110  giving  110    100    110
1    1      6            6      4      6 octal.
```

Hex, or hexadecimal, is even better from the programming point of view. One single hex digit will represent a number which uses up to four binary digits. This makes the system particularly suitable for modern microcomputers which use groups of eight, sixteen or thirty-two bits. Since a scale of sixteen is used, we need digits for 110 to 15, and the letters A to F are used, as Fig. C1 shows.

Denary	Hex
0	00
1	01
etc. to . . .	
9	09
10	0A
11	0B
12	0C
13	0D
14	0E
15	0F
16	10
17	11
etc.	

Figure C1. The hexadecimal scale for digits 0 to 15.

The conversions between hex and binary are particularly simple, as Fig.C2 shows. To convert hex to binary, write the equivalent four-bit binary number for each hex digit.

Hex	Binary	Hex	Binary
00	0000	08	1000
01	0001	09	1001
02	0010	0A	1010
03	0011	0B	1011
04	0100	0C	1100
05	0101	0D	1101
06	0110	0E	1110
07	0111	0F	1111

Figure C2.   Hex and binary scales.

For example, to convert Hex AF to binary, write down the codes 1010 for A and 1111 for F giving 10101111 as the binary equivalent.

To convert from binary to hex, group the binary digits into fours, starting from the right-hand side. Then write the corresponding hex digits, not forgetting any one, two or three digit group at the left-hand side.

For example: Binary 11001011011 is grouped as 110 0101 1011, so that in hex it is 6 5 B.

Signed numbers

For integer numbers of two bytes, the left-hand bit, bit 15 is used as a sign bit. This means that the number $0 \times 7FFF$ is the largest positive integer, denary 32767. The number 0×8000 is equivalent to -32768, the largest negative number. In denary terms, to find the equivalent of a negative number, subtract the number value from 65536, and then convert to octal, hex or binary. When converting back, a negative result should be converted in the same way.

For example, converting -76 gives $65536 - 76 = 65460$, which in hex is FFB4, and in octal is 177664. In binary, this is 1111111110110100. Converting the binary number 1100111101101011 into hex gives CF6B, octal 147553, and denary 53099, so that the number it represents is -12437.

D
ASCII Codes in Denary, Octal and Hex

	D = denary	S = symbol	O = octal	H = hex		

D	S	O	H	D	S	O	H
32		40	20	33	!	41	21
34	"	42	22	35	#	43	23
36	$	44	24	37	%	45	25
38	&	46	26	39	'	47	27
40	(	50	28	41	)	51	29
42	*	52	2a	43	+	53	2b
44	,	54	2c	45	–	55	2d
46	.	56	2e	47	/	57	2f
48	0	60	30	49	1	61	31
50	2	62	32	51	3	63	33
52	4	64	34	53	5	65	35
54	6	66	36	55	7	67	37
56	8	70	38	57	9	71	39
58	:	72	3a	59	;	73	3b
60	<	74	3c	61	=	75	3d
62	>	76	3e	63	?	77	3f
64	@	100	40	65	A	101	41
66	B	102	42	67	C	103	43
68	D	104	44	69	E	105	45
70	F	106	46	71	G	107	47
72	H	110	48	73	I	111	49
74	J	112	4a	75	K	113	4b
76	L	114	4c	77	M	115	4d
78	N	116	4e	79	O	117	4f
80	P	120	50	81	Q	121	51
82	R	122	52	83	S	123	53
84	T	124	54	85	U	125	55
86	V	126	56	87	W	127	57

88	X	130	58	89	Y	131	59
90	Z	132	5a	91	[	133	5b
92	\	134	5c	93	]	135	5d
94	^	136	5e	95	_	137	5f
96	'	140	60	97	a	141	61
98	b	142	62	99	c	143	63
100	d	144	64	101	e	145	65
102	f	146	66	103	g	147	67
104	h	150	68	105	i	151	69
106	j	152	6a	107	k	153	6b
108	l	154	6c	109	m	155	6d
110	n	156	6e	111	o	157	6f
112	p	160	70	113	q	161	71
114	r	162	72	115	s	163	73
116	t	164	74	117	u	165	75
118	v	166	76	119	w	167	77
120	x	170	78	121	y	171	79
122	z	172	7a	123	{	173	7b
124			174	7c	125	}	175	7d
126	~	176	7e	127	~	177	7f

Note: characters as shown here are as printed by an Epson RX–80 dot matrix printer. On-screen characters can differ in some cases, as can other printer characters.

Index

Notes